Women Only Works on Paper

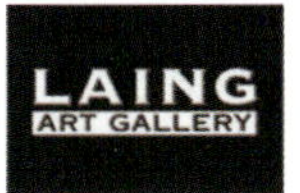

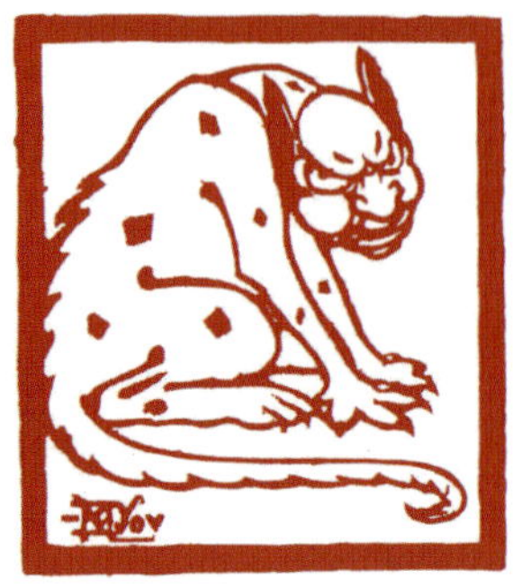

Acknowledgements:

An exhibition of this nature requires the assistance of a large number of
people, some of whom have contributed to the contextual notes.
We would especially like to thank:

Prudence and Rosalind Bliss	David Leighton
Quentin Bone	Eva Liss
Erika Brandl	Pauline Lucas
Elizabeth Bulkeley	Julie Milne
Sarah Bull	Conor Mullan
Christopher Campbell-Howes	Peter and Renate Nahum
Hermione Carline	Elle Nixon
Annie Davis	William Pryor
Daniel Dullaway	Michel and Susie Remy
Eleanor Durbin	Christina Rhys
Patrick Elliott	Sarah Richardson
Jane England	Jocelyn Sampson
Claire Fulleylove	Peyton Skipwith
Nicolas Granger-Taylor	Paul Stamper
Geoff Hassell of artbiogs.co.uk	Robert Travers
Richard Hodgson	Anne Ullmann
Mimi Jardine	Louise Walker
Simon Lawrence	Farang Wren

First published in 2021 by LISS LLEWELLYN

ISBN : 978-1-9993145-7-6

Text © Sacha Llewellyn, Alanna Jones, George Richards & multiple authors
Photography: Glynn Clarkson, Pierre Emmanuel Coste & Petra van der Wal

Design and Typesetting by David Maes
Printed by Zenith Media, March 2021

Women
Only
Works on Paper

For Rebecca

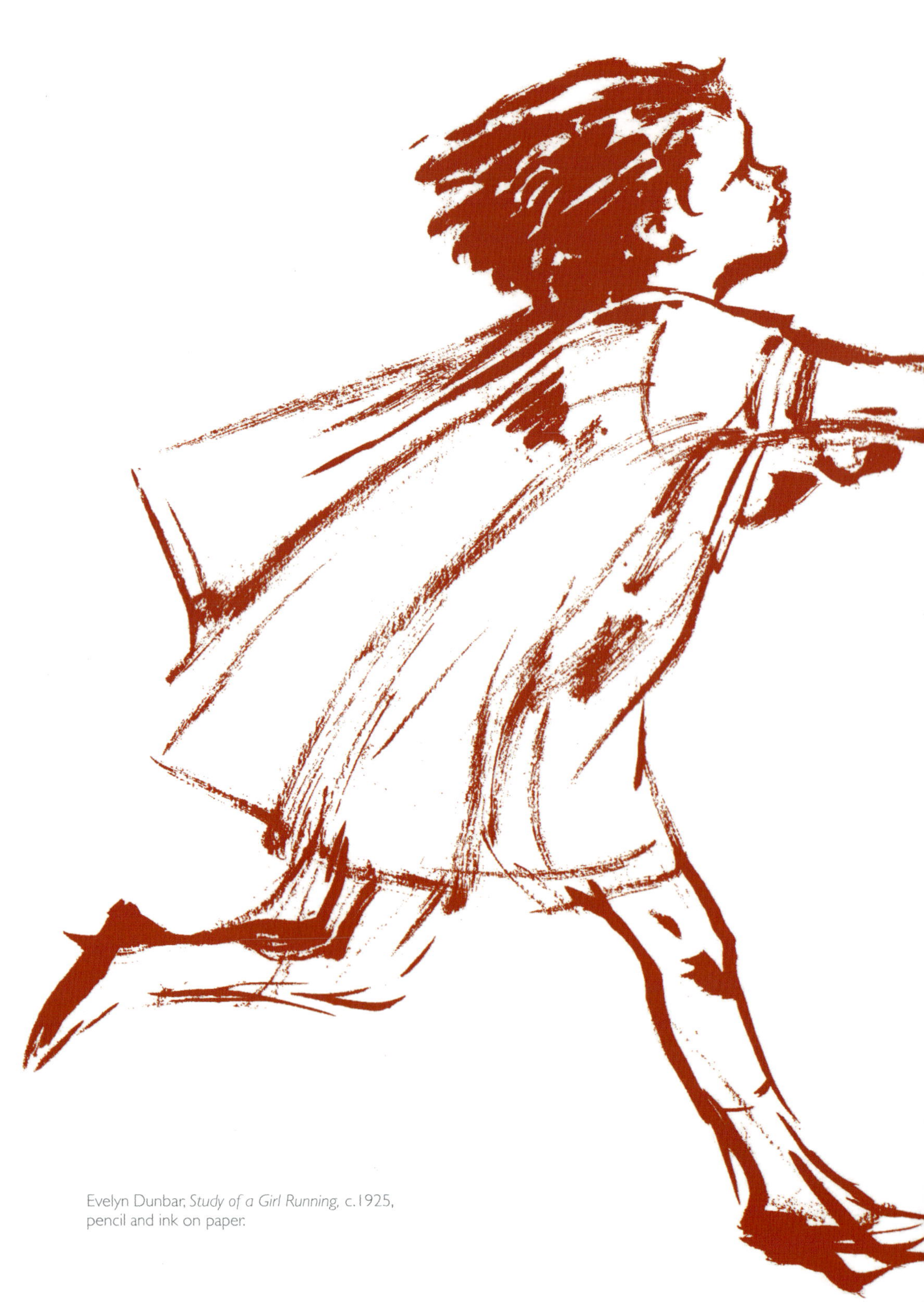

Evelyn Dunbar, *Study of a Girl Running*, c.1925, pencil and ink on paper.

CONTENTS

WOW !

Over the past years, I and my colleagues in the art team have made a conscious attempt to address the omissions and erasures that are inherent in public art collections like that of the Laing Art Gallery and indeed within the canon of British art itself. With a particular focus on gender, this has manifested itself in a series of exhibitions, redisplays of the permanent collection and a refocusing of our acquisitions policy. It is therefore opportune that we are able to work in partnership with Liss Llewellyn on *WOW: Women Only Works on Paper*. Liss Llewellyn have long made it their mission to encourage the reappraisal of some of the less well-known figures of 20th-century art – who more often than not are women. In particular, their impressive publications and exhibitions have brought many women artists more mainstream attention.

Liss Llewellyn have drawn together over fifty works on paper from private collections. The selection includes a wide variety of works in a range of styles and of outstanding quality. The artists Vanessa Bell, Hilda Carline, Ithell Colquhoun, Winifred Knights and Paule Vézelay are all represented, as well as other accomplished but less well-known artists. *WOW* will be shown concurrently with *Challenging Convention* which focuses on the work of Laura Knight, Gwen John, Vanessa Bell and Dod Procter.

The permanent collection is at the heart of our programming strategy, but unusually the Gallery was founded without a collection. In spite of this it has grown over the years with gifts, bequests and purchases by successive curators and is designated by Government as being of national if not international significance. The watercolour holdings are at the heart of this unique collection and are widely recognised as being of exceptional importance. Particularly strong in 18th- and 19th-century watercolours along with some important 20th-century works, all areas are represented in depth. There is amongst this a small but distinguished group of female artists, some of whom are shown in this exhibition, including Edna Clarke Hall, Annie French, Frances Hodgkins, Julia Beatrice How, Lucy Kemp-Welch, Thérèse Lessore and Gwen Raverat.

We are delighted to be working in collaboration with Liss Llewellyn and to have the opportunity to bring talented and largely 'unsung' 20th-century women artists to a wider audience. In particular at this moment in time when issues of gender equality have been highlighted by the pandemic it seems fitting that we reflect that many of these issues have not entirely disappeared and are only just beneath the surface. The exhibition, in spite of being modest in scale, really does do justice to its title – WOW ! indeed.

Julie Milne,
Chief Curator of Art Galleries, Tyne & Wear Archives & Museums

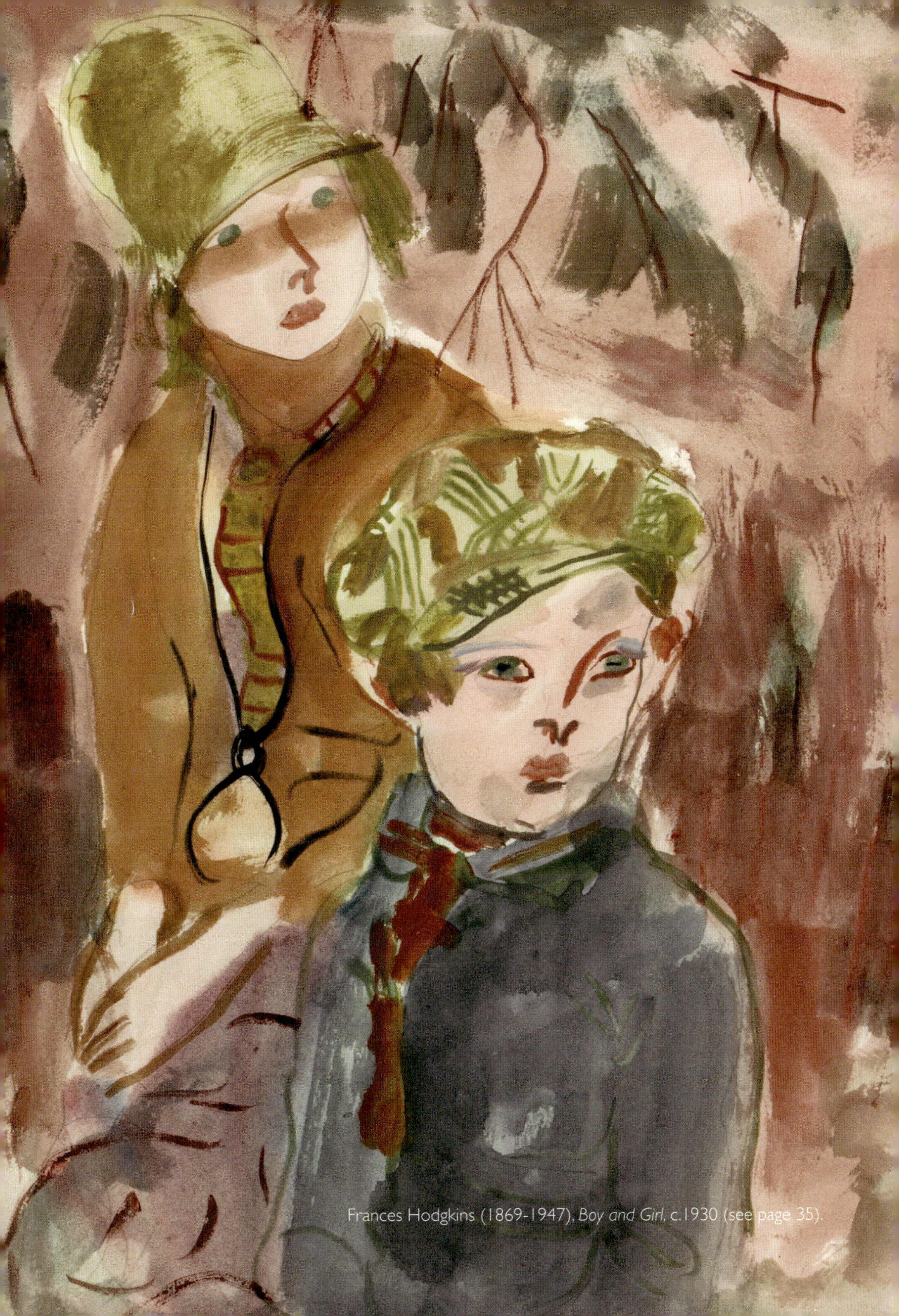

Frances Hodgkins (1869-1947), *Boy and Girl*, c.1930 (see page 35).

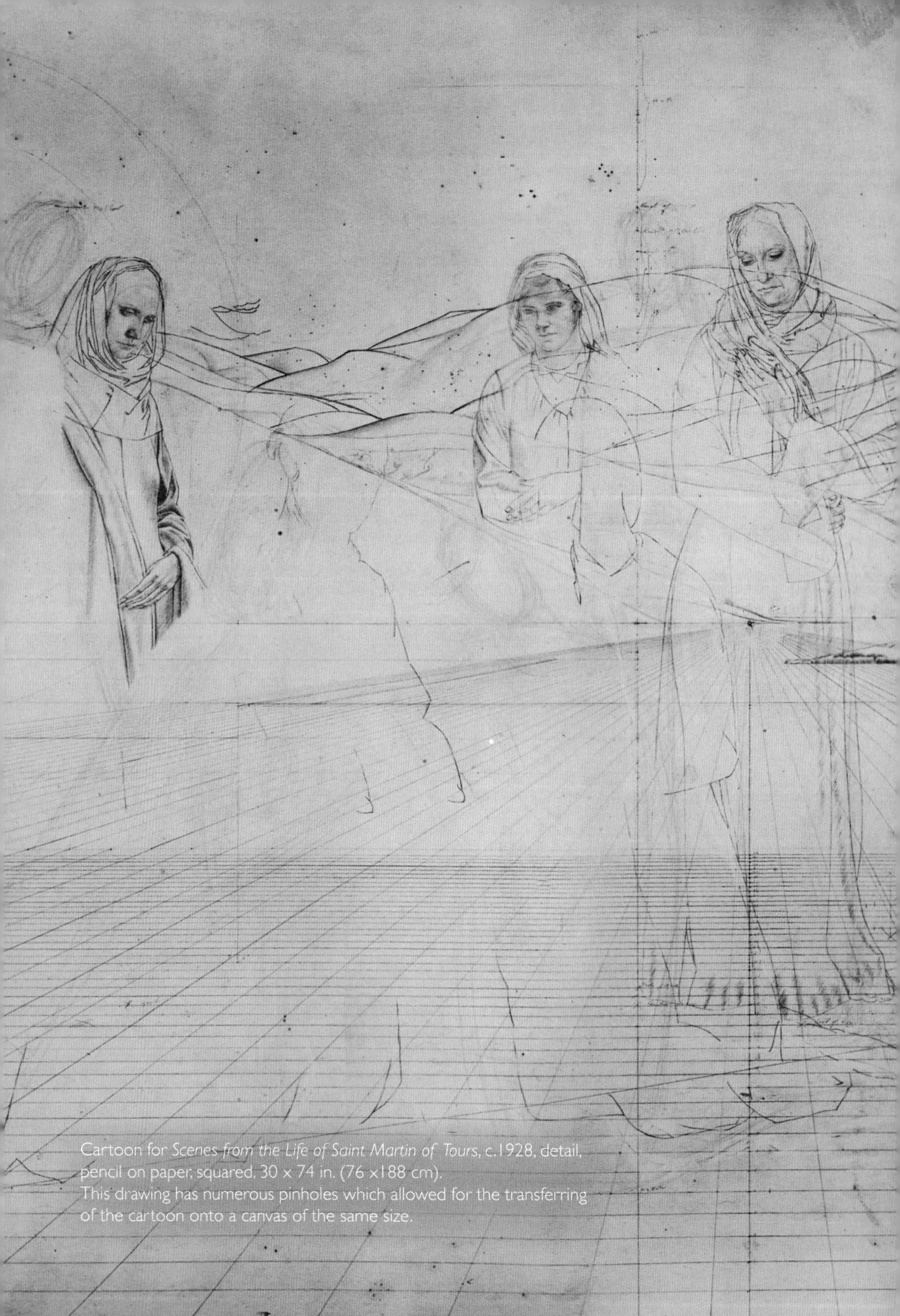

Cartoon for *Scenes from the Life of Saint Martin of Tours*, c.1928, detail,
pencil on paper, squared, 30 x 74 in. (76 x188 cm).
This drawing has numerous pinholes which allowed for the transferring
of the cartoon onto a canvas of the same size.

Drawn to Paper

Sacha Llewellyn

WOW – a collaboration between Liss Llewellyn and the Laing Art Gallery – showcases 38 British women artists working on paper between 1905 and 1975, a period of great change for women in the arts. The featured artists approached the medium in various ways, to transform paper into beautiful and complex works of art. The exhibition celebrates the diversity of these approaches and highlights the ways in which paper provided artists with a rich arena for artistic innovation.

Paper's adaptability allows for a multitude of techniques. Using paper in its traditional role as a support for drawings and prints, or creating collage and sculpture, artists responded to the medium's inherent qualities – malleable, smooth and sensuous – to test ideas, express feelings or create a finished work. It is often in the more formative moments that the works in this exhibition most resonate; through these studies we bear witness to the seed of an idea in germination, as in Clare Leighton's iconic *Southern Harvest*, or Evelyn Dunbar's celebrated works for the War Artists' Advisory Committee.

Selecting hand-made, mould-made or machine-made papers in various weights, textures and tints, according to their intentions, artists worked with a variety of media from pencil, ink and pastel, to watercolour, tempera and oil, sometimes incorporating extraneous elements such as gold leaf and metallic forms. Working on monumental sheets, such as Winifred Knights' cartoon for *Scenes from the Life of Saint Martin of Tours,* or tiny pages such as Edith Granger-Taylor's *Small Grey Abstract*, women's choices were nevertheless sometimes dictated by circumstance: the propensity of Frances Richards and Tirzah Garwood – by no means isolated cases – to work on paper on a small scale was in part a result of not having access to a studio.

From portraits, landscapes, botanical studies, abstracts, still lives and *genre* scenes, the works in *WOW* highlight the artists' skill and dexterity in drawing on paper, which was at the core of artistic training and practice. Some artists have used the traditional techniques of etching, screen printing and woodblock to create a diverse range of images. Others highlight the ethereal properties of paper through precise cuts, resulting in elaborate collages combining shapes, patterns and designs, or manipulate and compress paper to create inventive and surprising sculptures. Featuring both famous and lesser-known talents, *WOW* celebrates the many ways in which women artists expressed themselves through works on, and with paper and highlights their contribution to the graphic arts in 20th century Britain.

Marion Wallace-Dunlop (1864 -1942)

Marion Wallace-Dunlop exhibited her series of roaring and grinning 'Devils in Divers Shapes' at John Baillie's Gallery, London, in 1905. A review in *The Studio*, while admiring the originality and inventiveness of the prints, considered, nevertheless, that 'a feminine belief in the pretty is often apparent in them'. Knowledge of the artist's biography, which included daring protests for the women's suffrage movement, suggests a wider range of thematic and emotional content.

Trained at the Slade School of Fine Art, by the 1890s Wallace-Dunlop was enjoying a successful career as a painter and illustrator. After 1900, however, she turned her classical training to the service of the militant women's suffrage movement, joining the Central Society for Women's Suffrage, the Fabian Women's Group and the Women's Social and Political Union, for whom she organized and designed a series of spectacular processions. After being arrested for militancy in 1909, she became the first British suffragette to go on hunger strike.

With its intense glare, sharp claws and whip-like tail, this almost-amphibious and androgynous creature is perhaps the most menacing of the *Devils* series. In 1867, the writer and social critic Thomas Carlyle termed universal suffrage the "Devil- appointed way" to count heads. In this context, it is easy to imagine that Wallace-Dunlop fully intended for her devils to be the very incarnation of a sense of outrage at the injustices to which women were subjected.

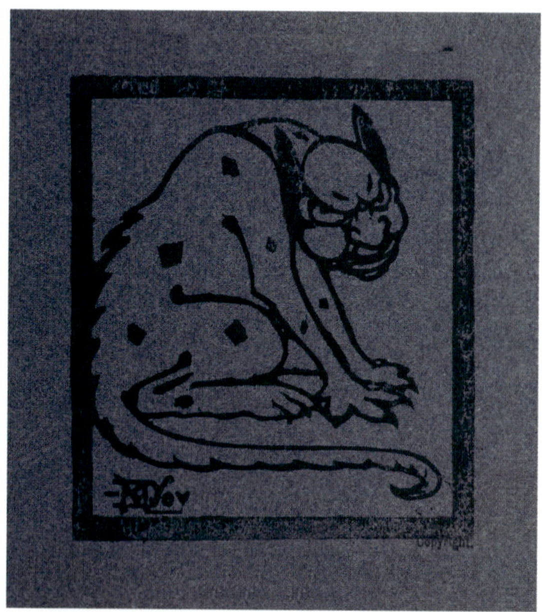

A Glaring Demon,
from *Devils in Divers Shapes,* c.1906,
signed with monogram, titled to reverse
woodcut proof on grey paper before colouring,
5 x 4 in. (12.8 x 10.2 cm).

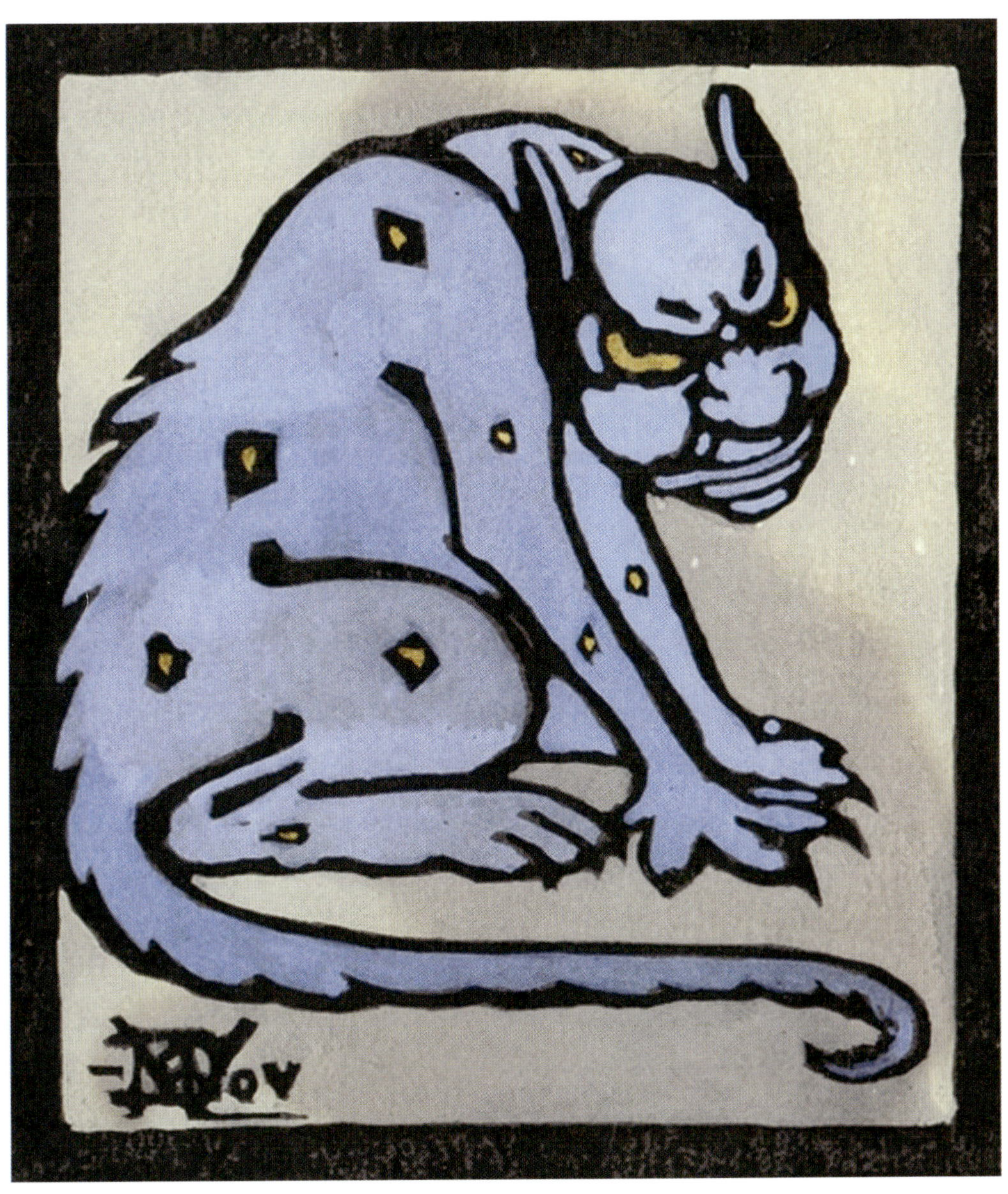

A Glaring Demon, (blue and yellow) from *Devils in Divers Shapes*, c.1906,
signed with monogram, titled to reverse
woodcut on grey paper with added colour, 5 x 4 in. (12.8 x 10.2 cm).

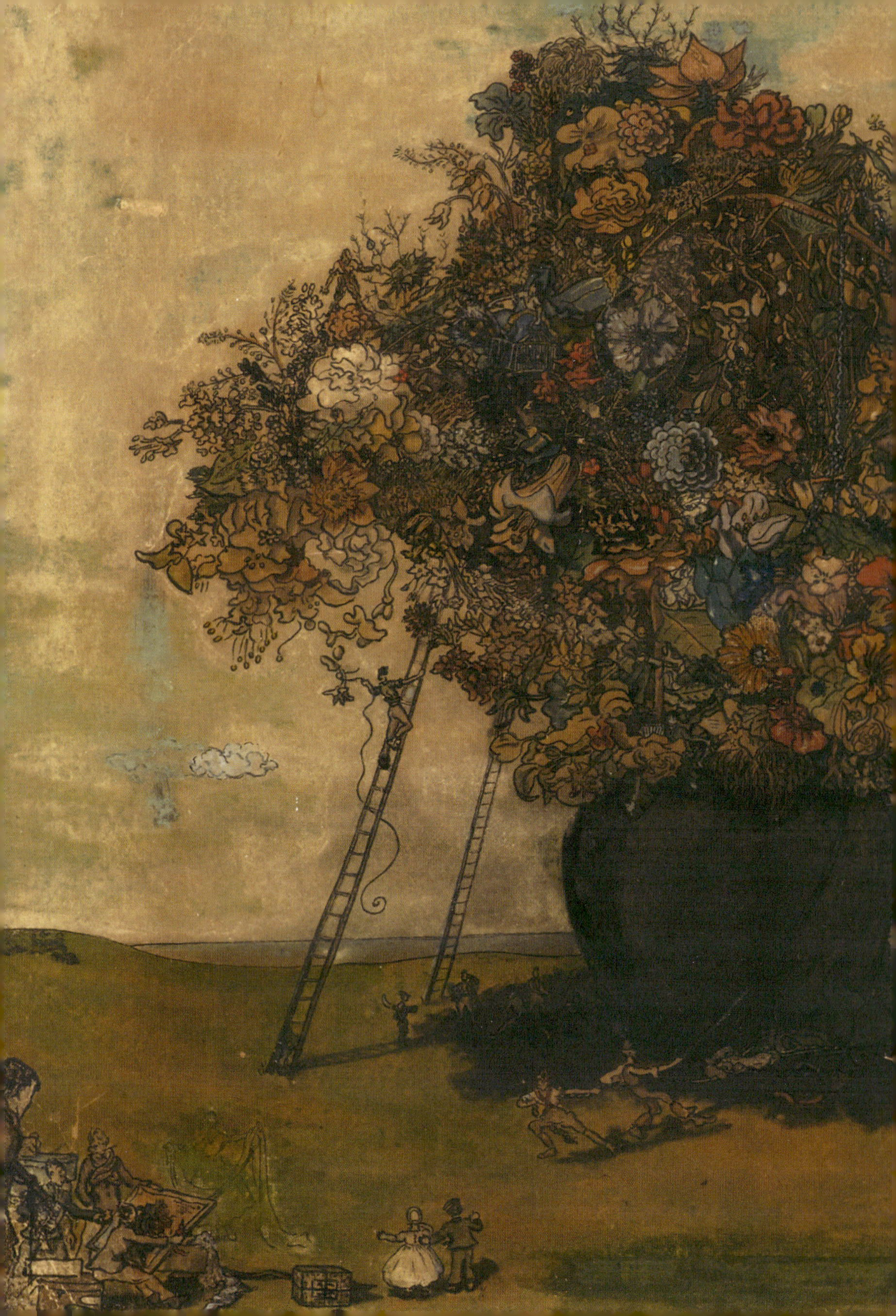

Nancy Nicholson (1899-1977)

In his book *Flower and Still Life Painting* (1928), Charles Holme considered that 'William Nicholson's popular reputation is that of a flower-painter above all' and that 'his work in this direction lies along the great line of tradition'. It is hardly surprising, therefore, that Nancy Nicholson has depicted her distinguished father, with her characteristic humour, painting a still life of flowers in a vase, any hint of spontaneity negated by the group of diminutive men on ladders carefully arranging the stems. In the corner, Nancy's husband Robert Graves, newly demobilized from the army, towers above the scene.

Of this work, the writer Candia McWilliam has commented, 'the language is satisfying in composition as one would expect of a printmaker, effective on contextualising and subversive levels as one would expect of a dedicated feminist, and richly, acutely seen, transmuting an apparent still life into a telling human dynamic'.

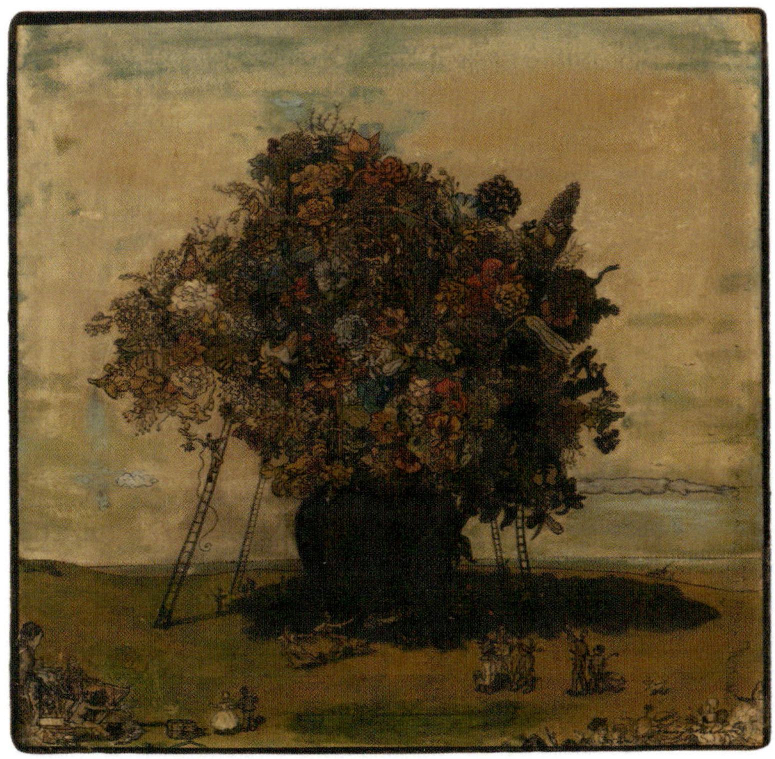

William Nicholson at Work, 1918, signed,
gouache on card, 14 ½ x 14 ½ in. (37 x 37 cm).

Hilda Carline (1889 -1950)

Hilda Carline met Gilbert Spencer while studying at the Slade School of Fine Art (1918–1922). Gilbert was the younger brother of Stanley, whom she went on to marry in 1925. These two portrait drawings, one executed in pencil, the other in red chalk, date to around 1919 and in their vigour and directness demonstrate the influence of the teachings of Professor Henry Tonks (1862-1937), who encouraged students to emulate the drawing methods of the Renaissance masters.

Pencil provided artists with the opportunity to create lines with a very precise delineation. Although red chalk could also be used in the same way, it tended to be valued primarily for its quality to convey subtle graduations in tone, similar to pastel and charcoal, ideal for the rendering of human flesh.

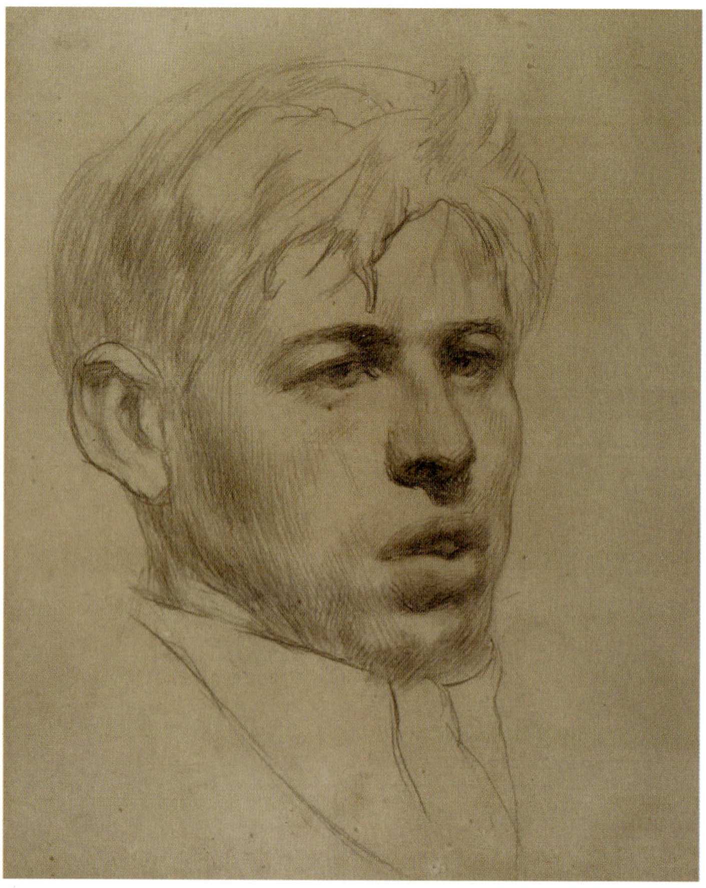

Portrait of Gilbert Spencer, c.1919,
pencil on paper, 17 ¾ x 11 ¾ in. (45 x 30 cm).

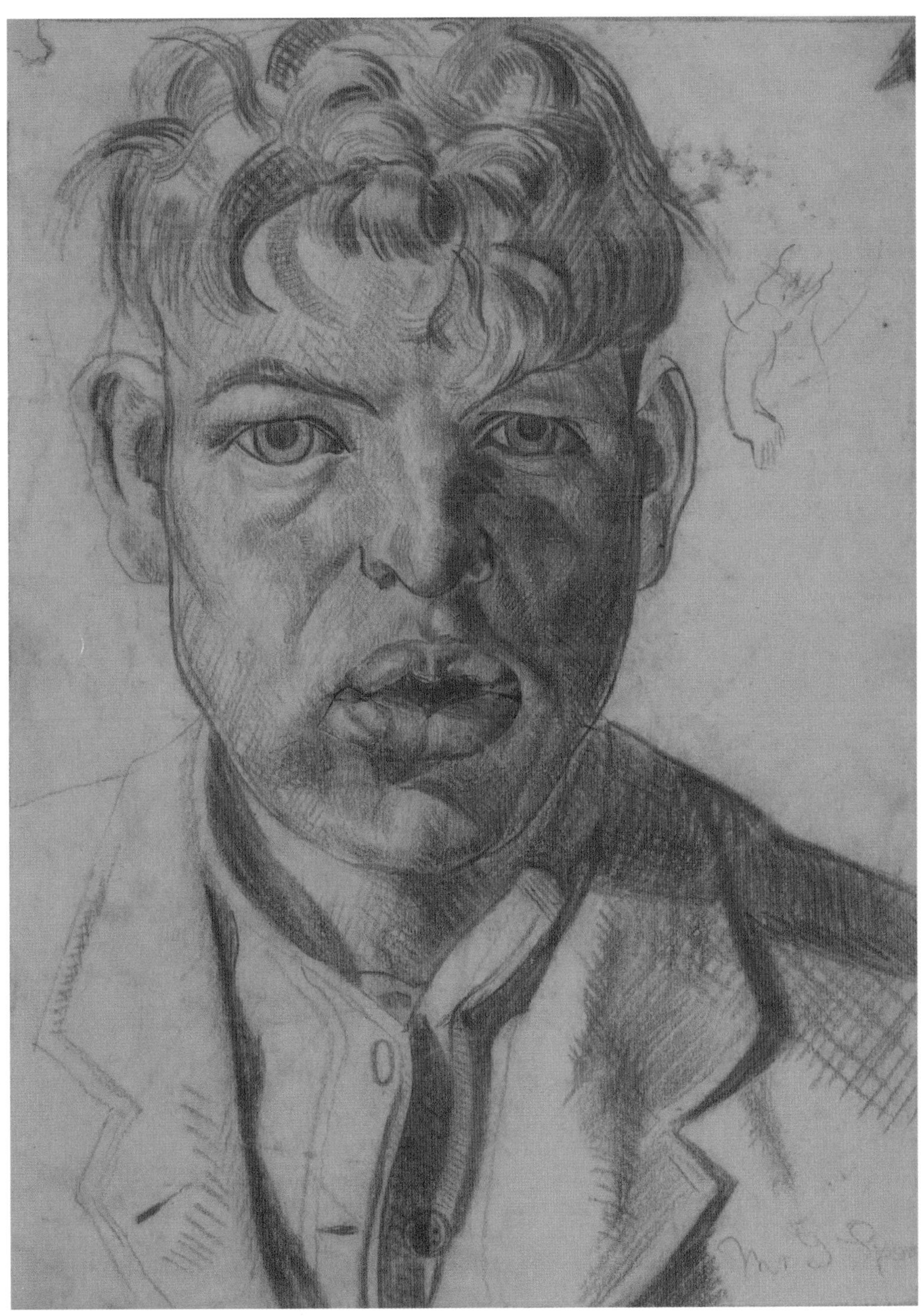

Portrait of Gilbert Spencer, c.1919, inscribed 'Mr G Spencer',
red chalk on paper, 11 ¾ x 11¾ in. (45 x 30 cm).

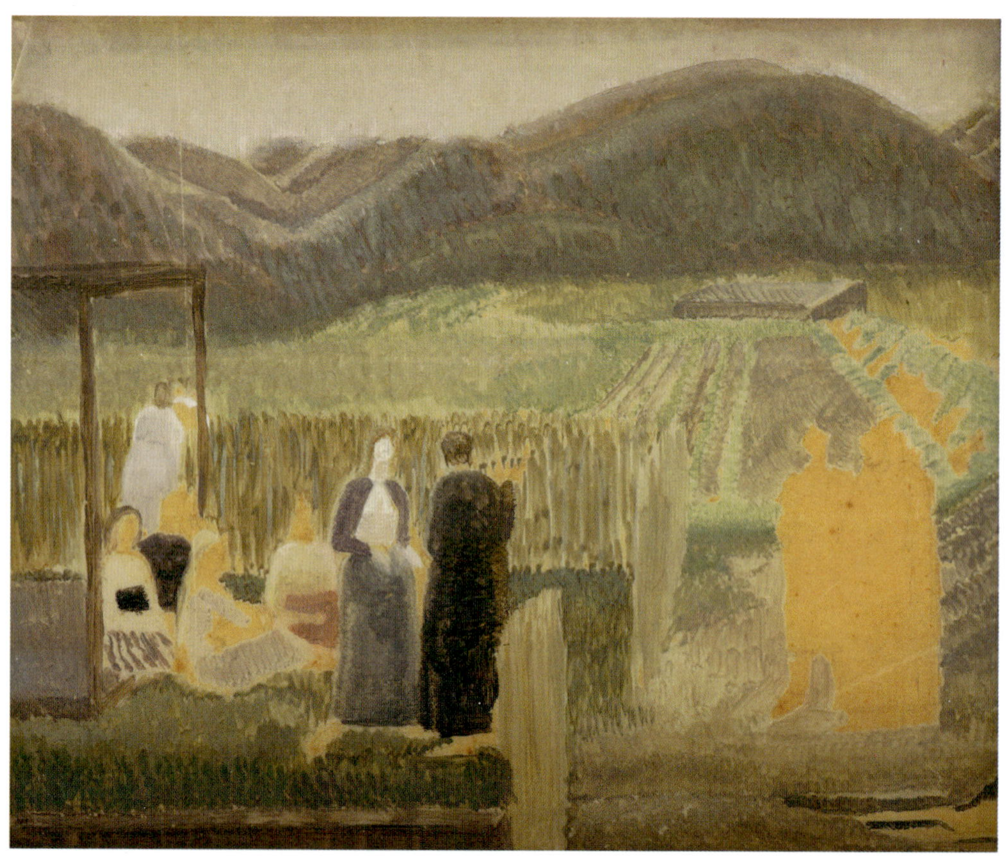

Paradise, 1921,
thinned oil on tracing paper, 7 ¼ × 8¾ in. (18.3 × 22 cm).

Colour study for foreground figure of woman combing her hair, *Santissima Trinita*, mid-1920s,
thinned oil over pencil on tracing paper on panel, 5 ½ × 6 ¼ in. (14 × 16 cm).

Writing to her mother about *Paradise* from the artist's colony of Anticoli Corrado (in the Latium) in 1921, Knights stated, '*I haven't thought about the figures properly, but I have all the landscape and all the colour . . .*' adding that she worked in the evenings '*partly because it is an evening effect, partly because it is too hot to struggle up the hill to it in the day*'.

Knights' letters indicate that as the painting evolved it underwent several changes – '*I keep on at my composition, rubbing out, rubbing it out. I will get it right soon. It's changed to the Annunciation now*'. A few months later Knights wrote: '*I have got another subject now, Abigail, same background*'.

Paradise is untraced and may never have been completed. The planned size, which was identical to Knights' Rome Scholarship winning entry, *The Deluge*, suggests that Knights intended to submit the painting to the Rome School Faculty as her major first-year work.

The theme of *Paradise* is close in spirit to Knights' Rome School *chef-d'oeuvre*, *The Santissima Trinita* (1924-30), which depicts women resting in a field during a pilgrimage to the sanctuary at Vallepietra in the Lazio. This study of a woman combing her hair was drawn and worked up in colour on tracing paper so that it could be transferred to the final canvas. Thinned oil was used by Knights as an alternative to gouache and allowed her to anticipate colour combinations as they would appear in the final painting.

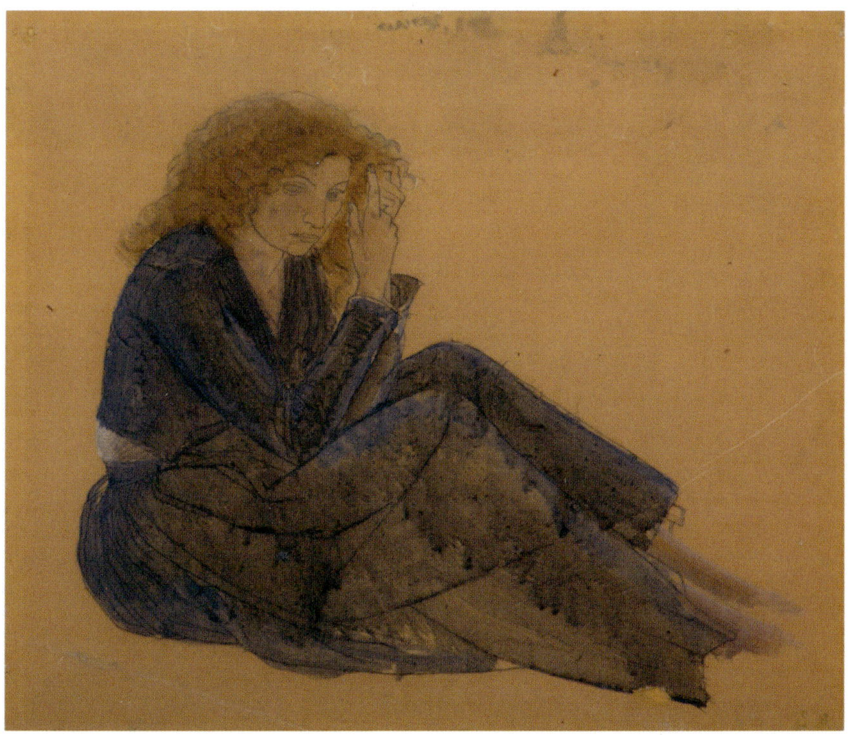

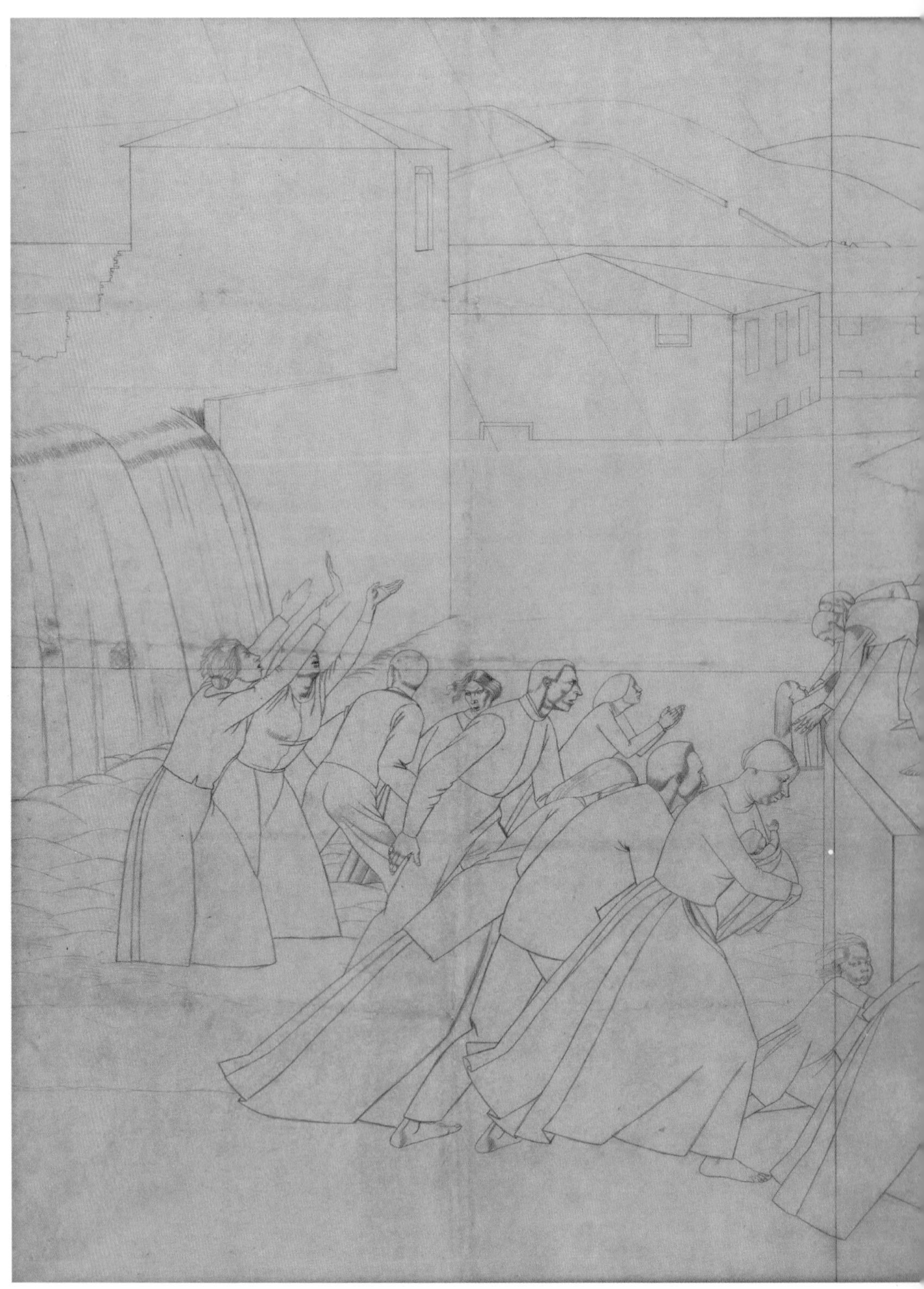

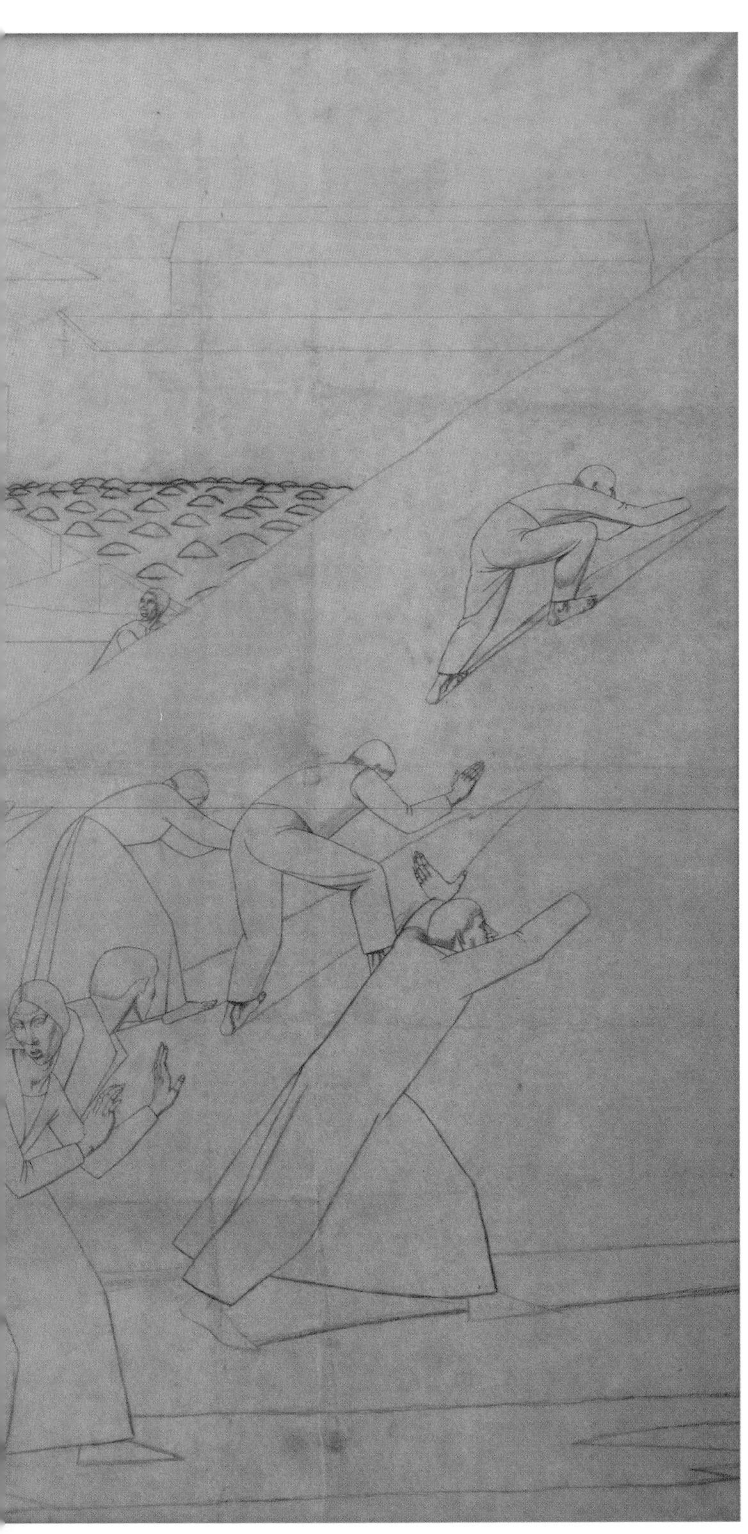

The original cartoon for
The Deluge, 1920,
pencil on tracing paper,
60 x 72 in. (152.4 x 183 cm).

The Deluge was Winifred Knights'
winning entry for the Prix de
Rome in 1920. On this full-size
cartoon, the lines are heavily
scored into the tracing paper
so that the outline could be
transferred onto the same size
canvas – now one of the prize
possessions of Tate Britain.

Julia Beatrice How (1867-1932)

A woman is engrossed in the pages of a newspaper, with a small table beside her bed serving to establish the foreground space. The artist has layered fragile strokes of pastel, creating a luminous quality to the woman's skin. The scene is lit by bright daylight, seemingly from a window out of sight on the left, and the artist has placed bright blue behind the figure to strikingly set off the pale hues of the sketched figure. Beatrice How (she dropped her first name of Julia) was born in Devon, England. She began studying in Paris at the prestigious Académie Delécluse in about 1893. She subsequently lived in France where she exhibited extensively, also showing some works at the Royal Academy of Arts in London. After 1910, How concentrated on studies of women and children in interiors, becoming best known for this type of subject.

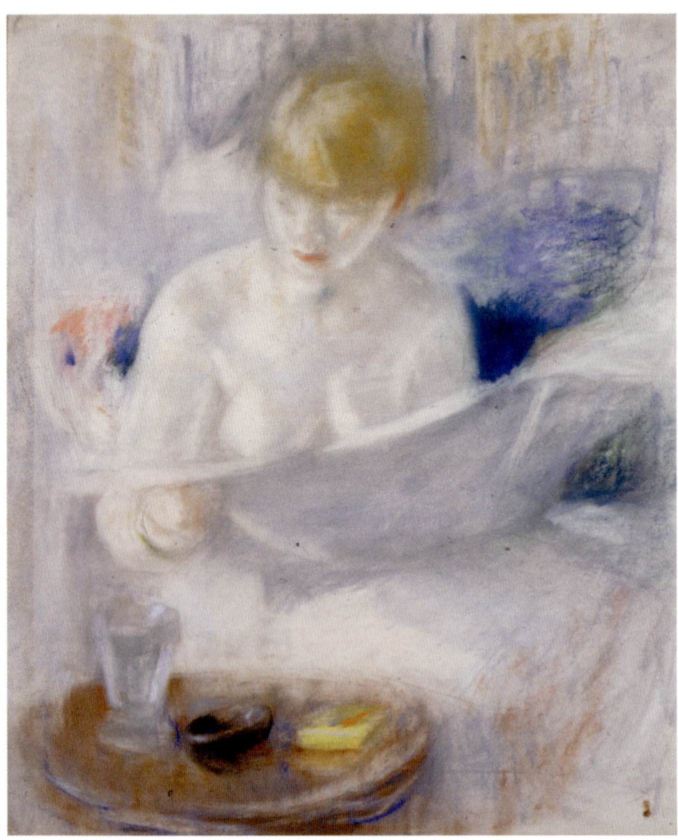

Lisant Dans le Lit (*Reading in Bed*), after 1910,
pastel and pencil on board,
25 ½ x 21 in. (64.8 x 53.5 cm). Purchased 1935.

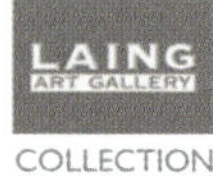

COLLECTION

This is one of a series of illustrations of Emily Brontë's novel *Wuthering Heights* made by Edna Clarke Hall. After studying at the Slade School of Art and Slade School of Fine Art and winning many prizes, Clarke Hall's artistic identity came into conflict with her husband's expectations of her role as a wife, leading to a breakdown in 1919. However, by 1922, she was exhibiting again. Catherine Earnshaw's yearning for Heathcliffe in the novel resonated with the artist's own sense of isolation. In this bleak landscape, the boats perhaps stand for the artist's desire for emotional escape. An art critic from the *Times* described Clarke Hall in 1926 as the 'most imaginative artist we have'. Clarke Hall was also a poet and had several volumes published in the 1920s and 1930s. In 1932 her husband was knighted for his work in reforming child law and she became Lady Clarke Hall.

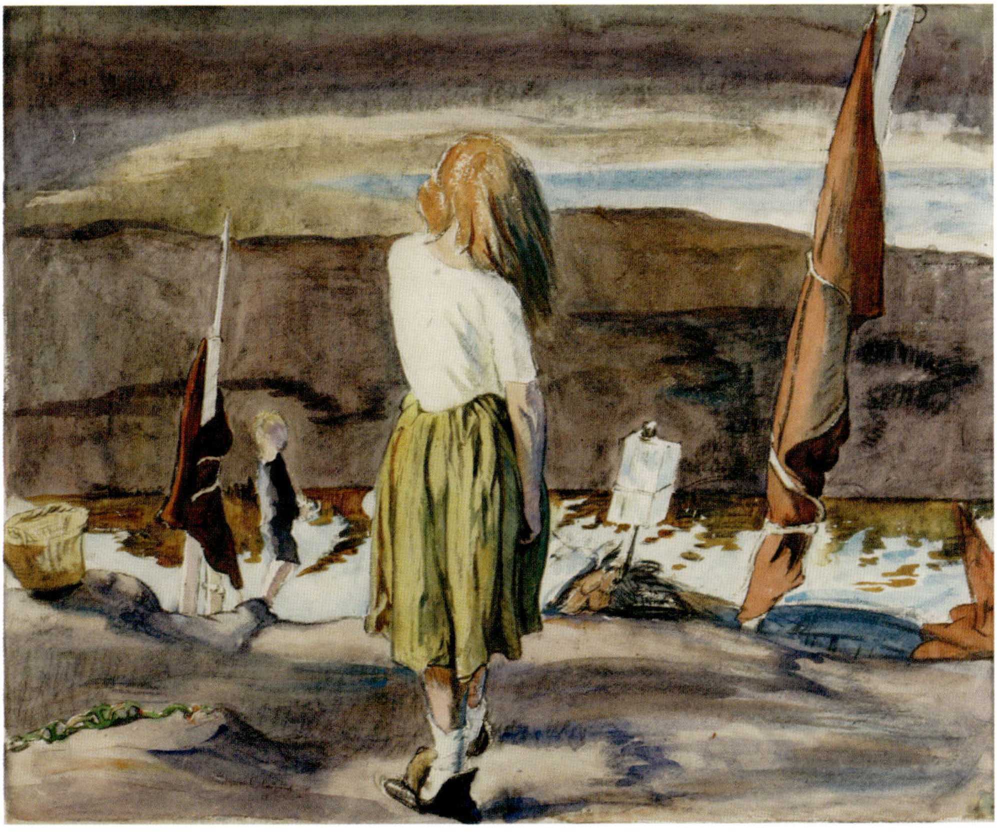

Catherine, c.1924, signed,
watercolour on paper.
Given by the Walker Mechanics Institute, 1942.

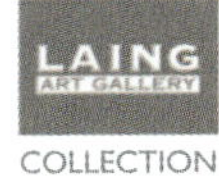

Phyllis Dodd (1899-1995)

Phyllis Dodd received a Royal Exhibition Scholarship to attend the Royal College of Art (RCA) for four years, from 1921-25, alongside Henry Moore (1898-1986), Raymond Coxon (1896-1997) and Edna Ginesi (1902-2000). In 1924, having achieved her Painting Diploma in two years (rather than three), she embarked on a Scholarship in etching and aquatint, under Frank Short. One of her earliest etchings – *The Beret* – shows a fellow student, Pindi, the pet name for Kathleen Bridle (1897-1989), who attended the RCA from 1921-25. Bridle went on to work as a glass painter in the Dublin studio of Harry Clarke and became one of the founders of the Ulster Unit in 1934. Frank Short insisted on draughtsmanship of the highest order as a prerequisite for entry to his course but this offered no barrier to Dodd, who in her fourth and final year won the drawing prize in the School of Painting. A confident self-portrait, dating to 1925, shows how well she mastered etching. The surviving drawing for the drypoint shows the process by which an image was first conceived on paper and then engraved on to the copper plate, which when printed appears in reverse. Unfortunately, she produced no more prints after leaving college despite Short's advice that she should concentrate on etching portraits because she was so fluently skilled in these. It was good advice at the time, but after the Wall Street crash, interest in this medium collapsed and never really recovered.

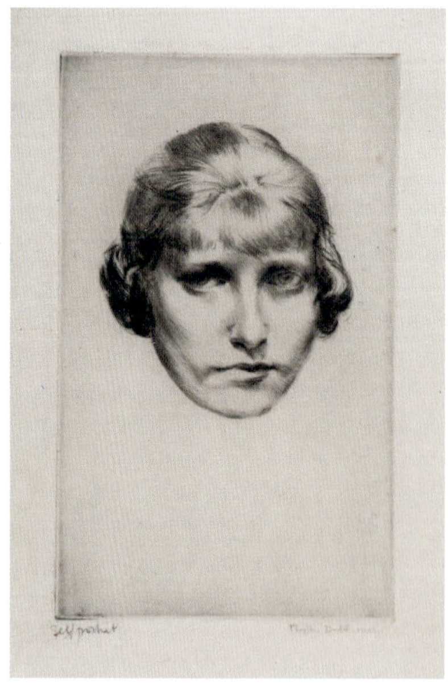

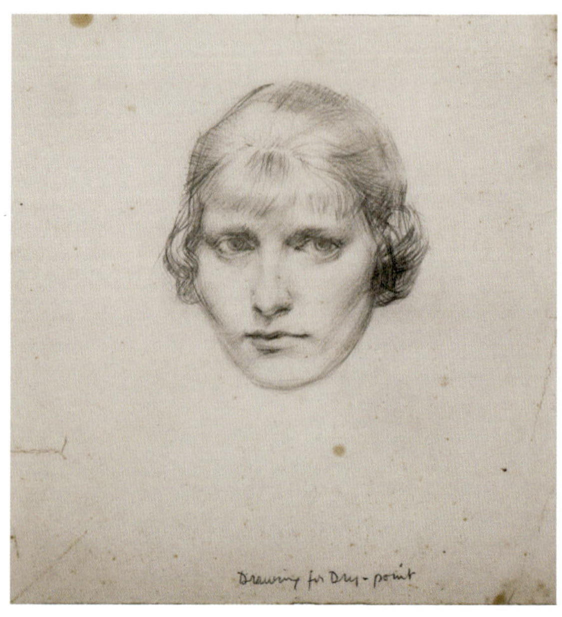

Self-portrait, 1925, signed & inscribed with title,
drypoint on paper,
paper size: 9 x 5 ½ in. (23 x 14 cm),
plate size: 7 x 4 in. (18 x 10 cm).

Self-portrait, 1925, inscribed 'Drawing for Dry-point',
pencil on paper, 9 x 8 ¾ in. (23 x 21.5 cm).

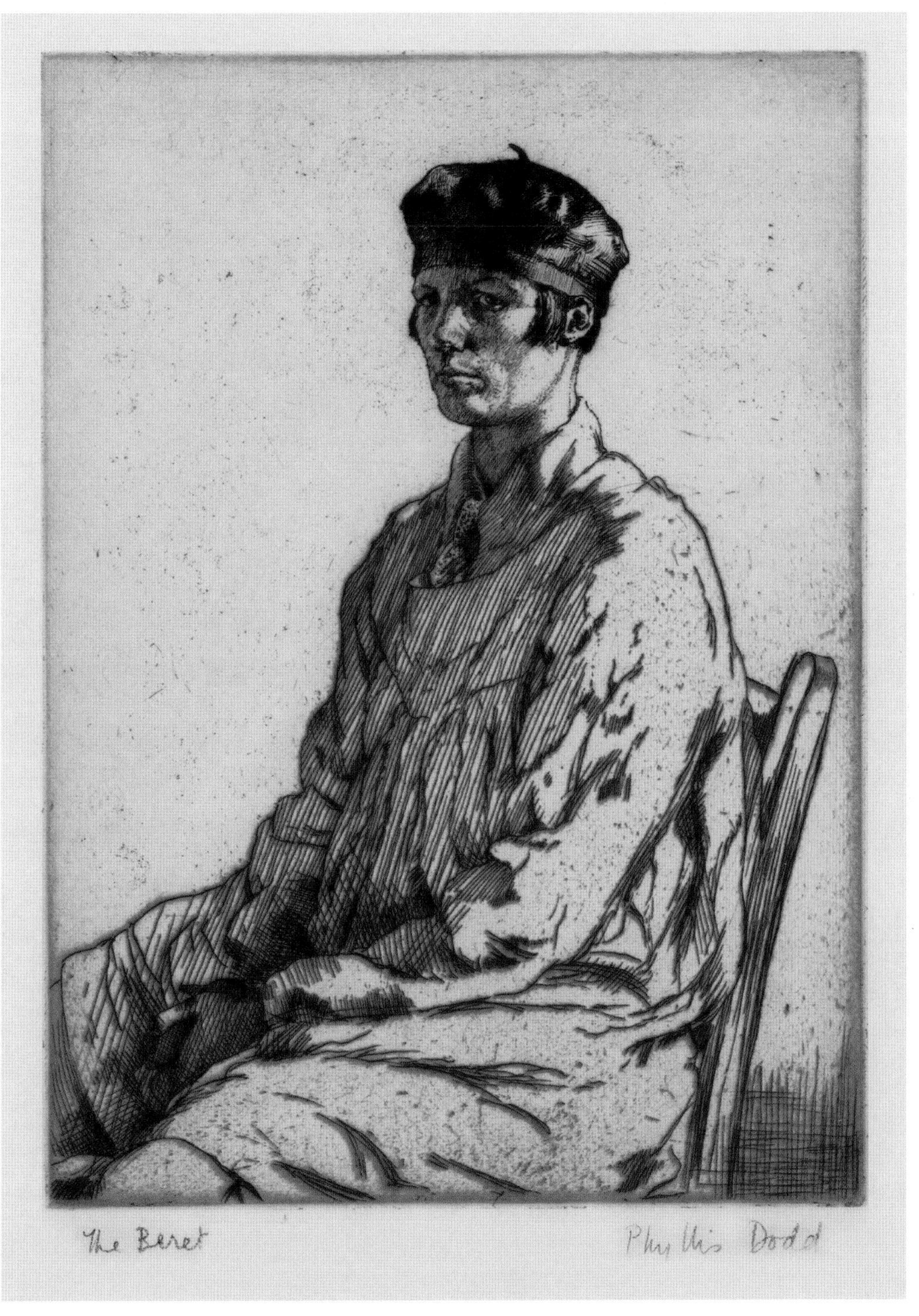

The Beret (Pindi), 1924, signed and inscribed with title, drypoint on paper,
paper size: 15 × 10 ¾ in. (38.2 × 27.5 cm), plate size: 8 ½ × 6 in. (21.5 × 15 cm).

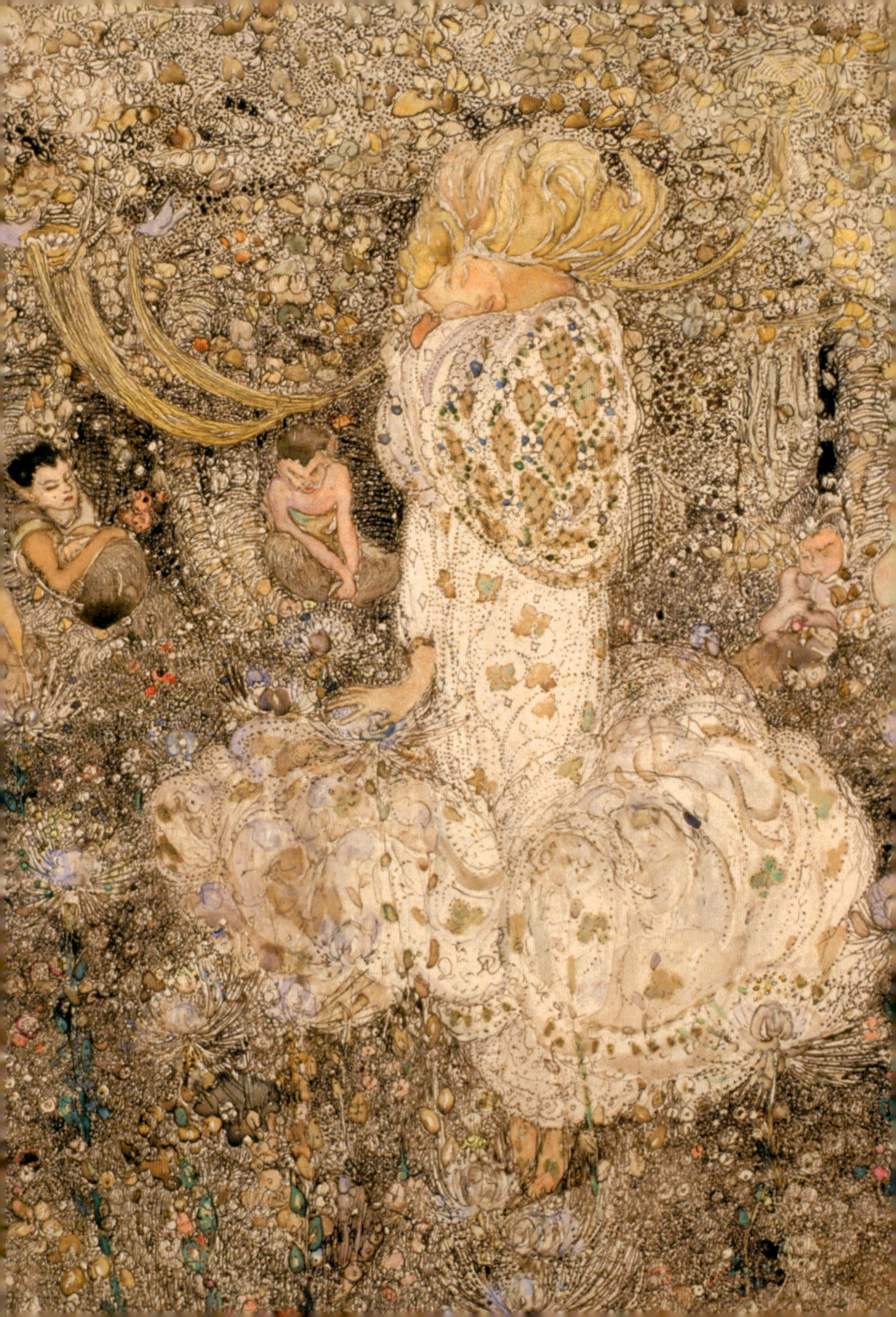

Annie French (1872-1965)

Fairies frequently featured as the subject of Annie French's work. The highly patterned nature of this piece indicates her interest in romantic and decorative imagery. The intricate details of her paintings were achieved through a combination of fine dots, hatching, and lines. Despite the small scale of her works, French's distinctive style gained her recognition at the Royal Academy. She had studied at the Glasgow School of Art and subsequently taught ceramic decoration there, from 1908 to 1912. French was also associated with the Glasgow School group of artists, whose Art Nouveau-inspired work stood in opposition to the historical and neo-classical styles which predominated in the Academies. The group promoted the idea that art and design should be an integral part of daily life. The precise dating of French's work is difficult because her signature style changed little during the course of her career.

'Pen and ink' is a drawing technique involving the use of black and other coloured inks where a fine line, as opposed to a broad line (such as achieved with charcoal and pastel), is sought. It was especially favoured as a medium for producing intricate designs.

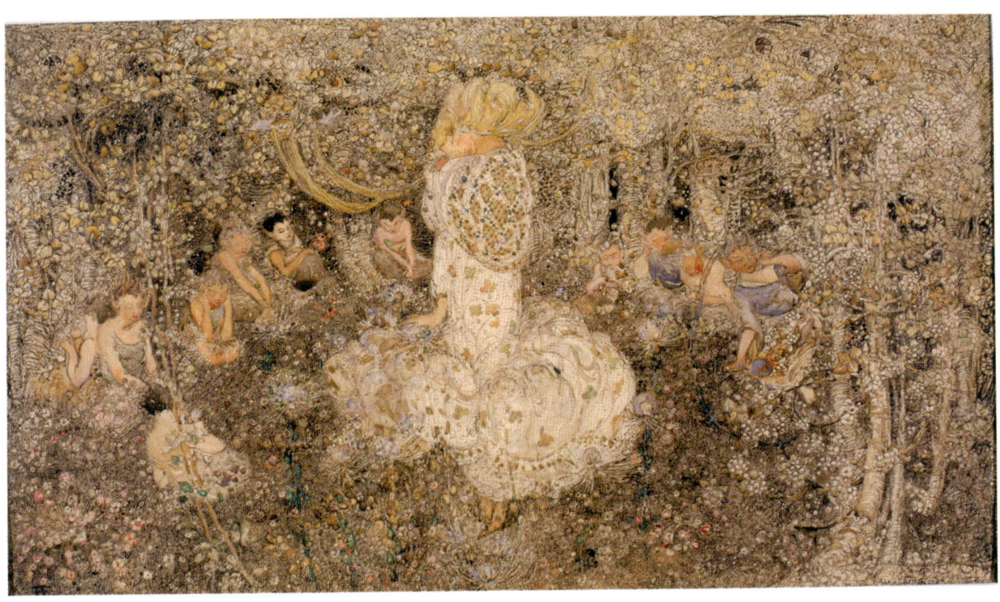

The Lady Under Enchantment, c. 1905-25, signed in monogram,
watercolour and pen & ink on paper, 12 x 15 ¾ in. (30.5 x 40.2 cm).
Given by Alex MacRae, 1954.

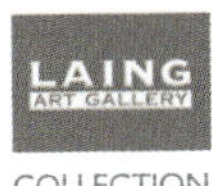

Gwen Raverat (1885-1957)

The Princess Lost, No 1 was produced by Gwen Raverat as an illustration for *The Wild Swans* by the well-known Danish author Hans Christian Andersen. As a trial proof, it differs from the final editioned version in which various details were further refined and the proportions of the composition altered. The fairy-tale stories were popular in the mid-1920s in Britain, their escapism providing reassurance at a time when the country was experiencing economic crises and social unrest. Raverat created this scene with simple yet evocative white lines cut out of a black background. She trained at the Slade School of Fine Art in London, and later played a fundamental role in modernising the technique of wood engraving in Britain. In the ten years between *The Princess Lost* and *Whoop for the Runaway* there is a marked evolution in the artist's style as she moved towards a greater economy of line and design, exploiting the qualities of wood engraving to their fullest potential. Raverat was especially interested in children's fiction and most of her book illustrations were produced from the 1930s. She spent most of her life in Cambridge and her childhood home is now situated within Darwin College, University of Cambridge, named after her grandfather, the great naturalist Charles Darwin.

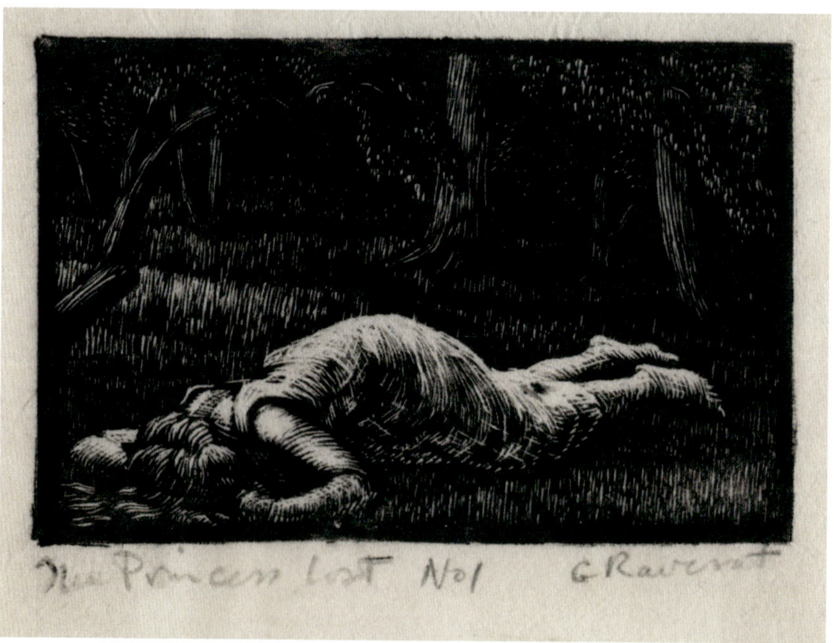

The Princess Lost, No 1 (trial proof), 1926, signed,
wood engraving on paper, 2 ¾ × 3 ½ in. (7 × 9 cm).
Bequeathed by J Thomas through the Art Fund 2015

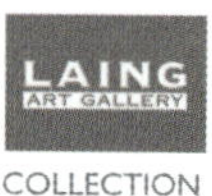

COLLECTION

Whoop for the Runaway, 1936,
wood engraving on paper, 2 × 3 in. (5.2 × 8.1 cm).

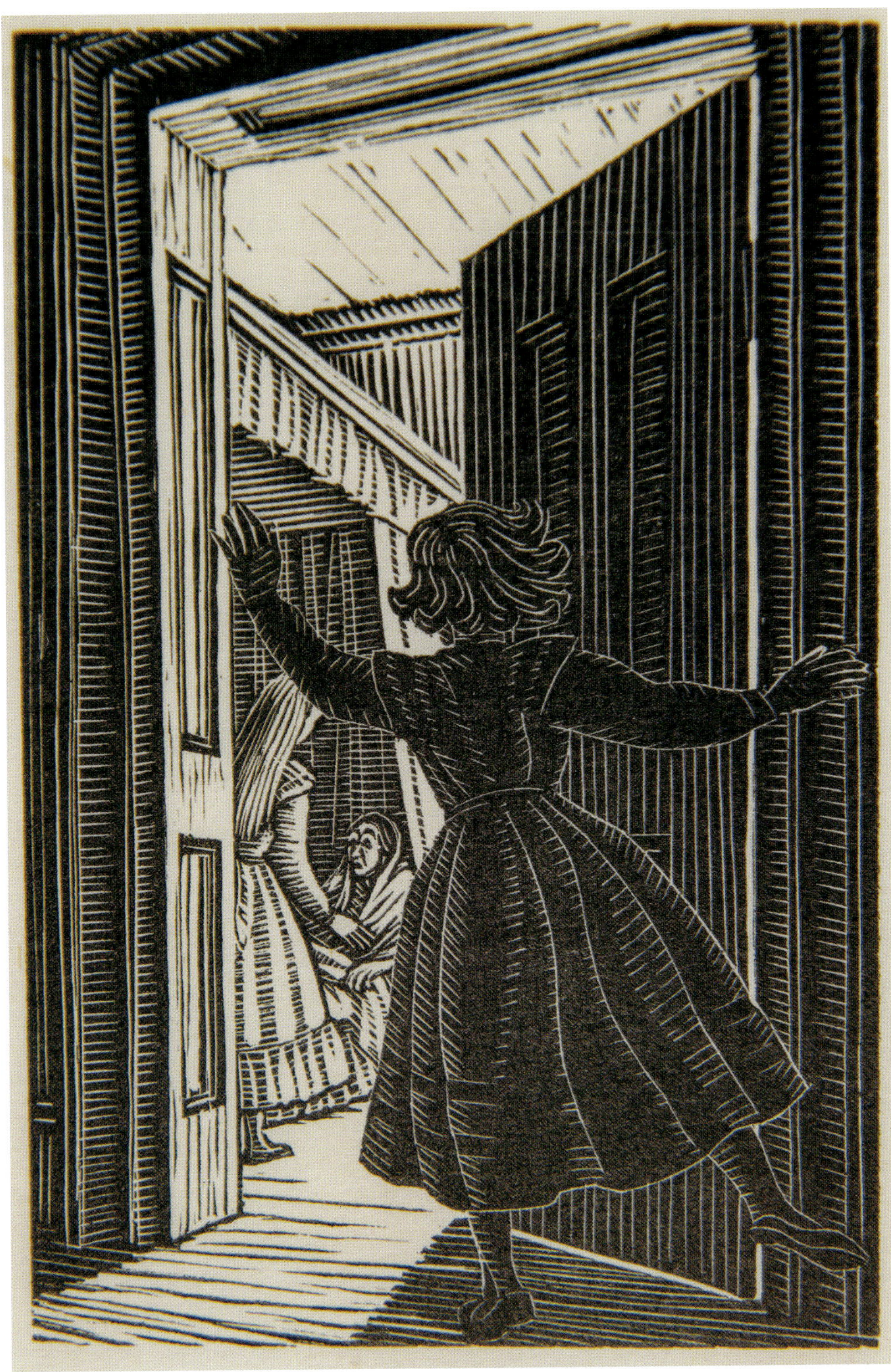

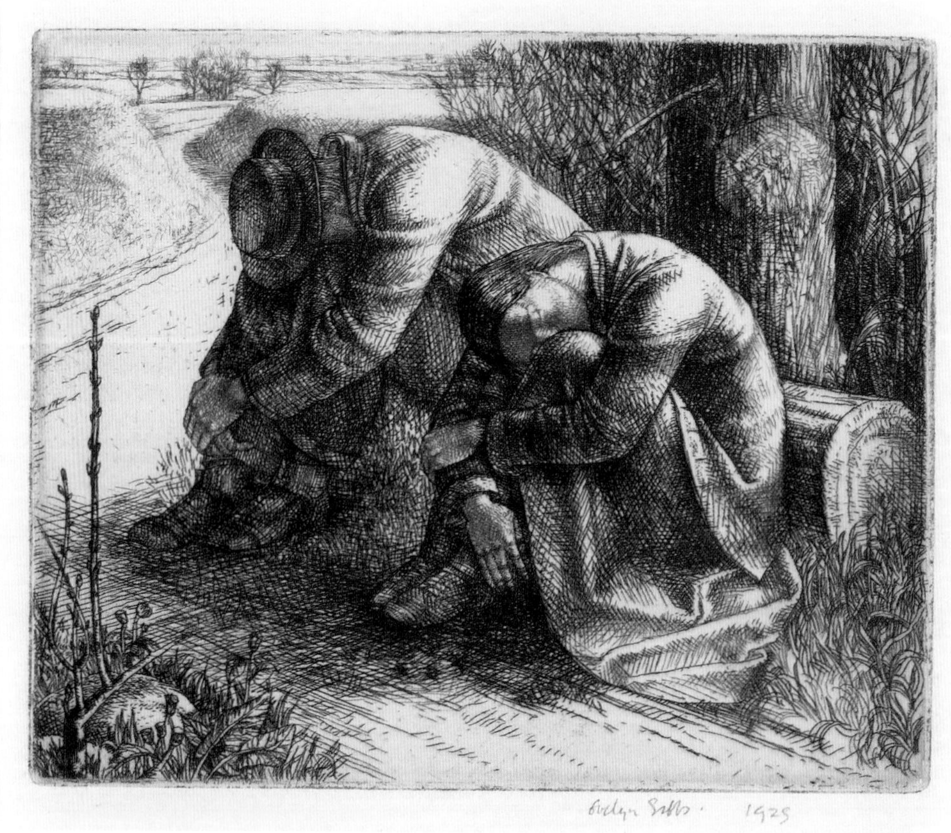

The Road, 1929, signed in pencil and dated,
etching on paper, 4 x 4 ¾ in. (10.2 x 12 cm).

Evelyn Gibbs' *Self-portrait*, made whilst at the Royal College of Art in 1927, a year before she applied for and won the coveted Rome Scholarship in Engraving, has much in common with, and might have been inspired by, Henry Fuseli's *Self-portrait* of 1770. Gibbs confidently shows herself at the start of the process of producing a drypoint, the blank copper etching plate on which she is working soon to become the self-portrait we are looking at. The drypoint medium, (made with a needle to create a soft burr giving a characteristic velvety appearance), was a more immediate method of printmaking than etching (where acid is used to deepen the lines on the plate). Generally fewer prints can be pulled in the case of drypoint as the plate gets too worn. An etching, such as *The Road*, might typically be made in an edition of up to 50 prints.

The Road resulted in her election as associate of the Royal Society of Painter-Printmakers, in 1929, the year she won her Rome Scholarship. A review described it as 'a beautiful little etching "The Road", with it's emotional significance – two tramps, a man and a woman are sitting crouched by the roadside, their heads upon their knees, utterly tired out – but the sunny road winds on through banked meadows away over the country …this etching promises well for Miss Gibbs' future, more even than her accomplished line engravings.'

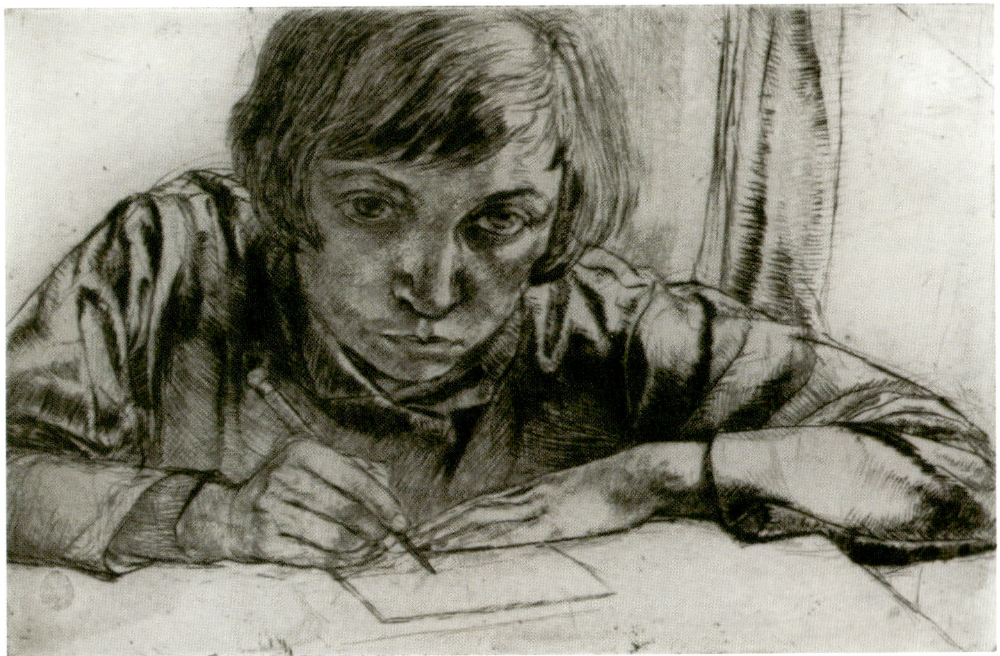

Self Portrait, 1927,
drypoint on paper, numbered in pencil, blind stamp lower right, plate size: 3 ¾ × 5 in. (8.6 × 12.7 cm), printed posthumously by the Executor of the Artist's Estate in an edition of 60.

Thérèse Lessore (1884-1945)

Thérèse Lessore found great enjoyment in displays of popular entertainment. She visited and sketched fairs with her second husband, the Camden Town artist Walter Sickert, whom she married in 1926. In the 1920s and 1930s, Lessore also produced many paintings of Swallow's Circus in Islington, London. Like many other artists of the time, her choice to depict ordinary entertainments was to some extent a conscious rejection of classical subject matter. In this watercolour, Lessore emphasised the decorative qualities of the rides and the patterns of the fairground awnings and fencing. The bright colours give an impression of the energy of the fairground experience.

Old Woman, an image of an old woman huddled into a corner, captures a moment of exhaustion. She faces away from the busy crowd underneath the railway arches, as if to signal her alienation from modernity. Lessore came from an artistic family, and the atmosphere of the household has been described as 'ambitious and creative'. Her father, Jules Lessore, was a painter and etcher, perhaps influencing Thérèse's decision to create a series of etchings. From 1904 to 1909, she studied at the Slade School of Fine Art, where she won the Melville Nettleship Prize for Figure Composition. In 1913, she founded the London Group with her then husband Bernard Adeney. She had her first solo exhibition in 1918 at the Eldar Gallery, London.

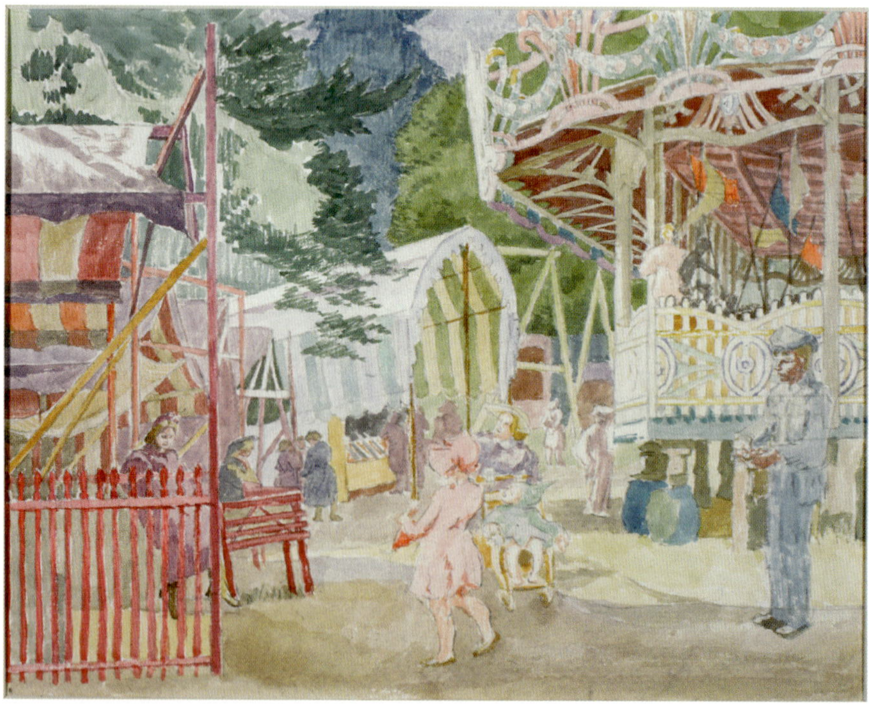

The Fair at Bath, about 1925-30,
watercolour on paper, 10 × 12 ¾ in. (25.6 × 32.2 cm).
Bequeathed by Thérèse Lessore and the Sickert Trust 1948.

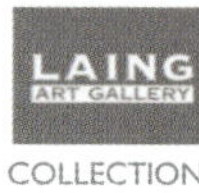

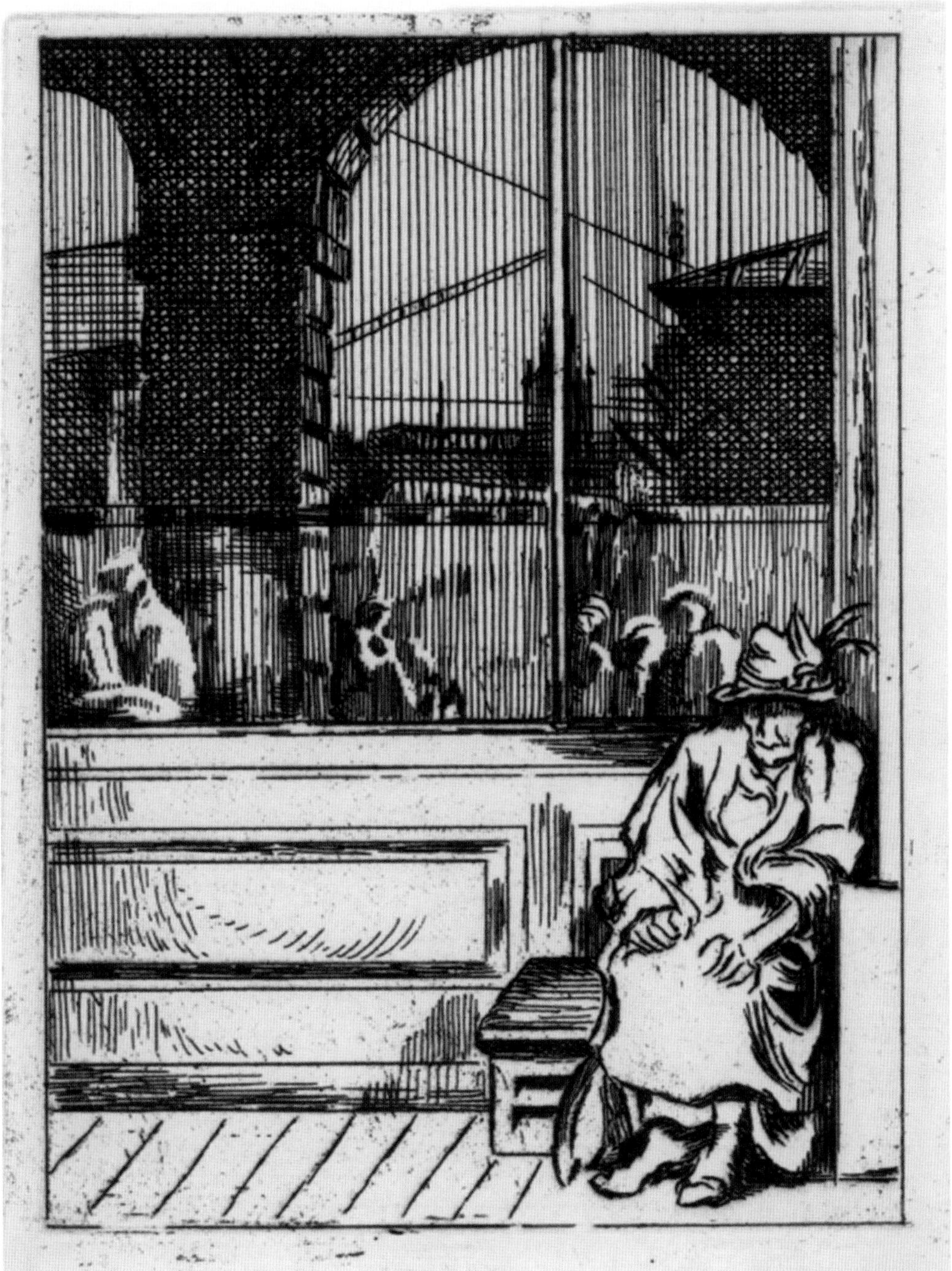

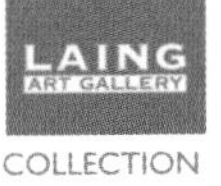

Old Woman,
etching on paper, image: 6 × 4 ¼ in. (15.1 × 11.1 cm) paper: 8 ¾ × 6 ½ in. (22.5 × 16.3 cm).
Given by the Sickert Trust 1948.

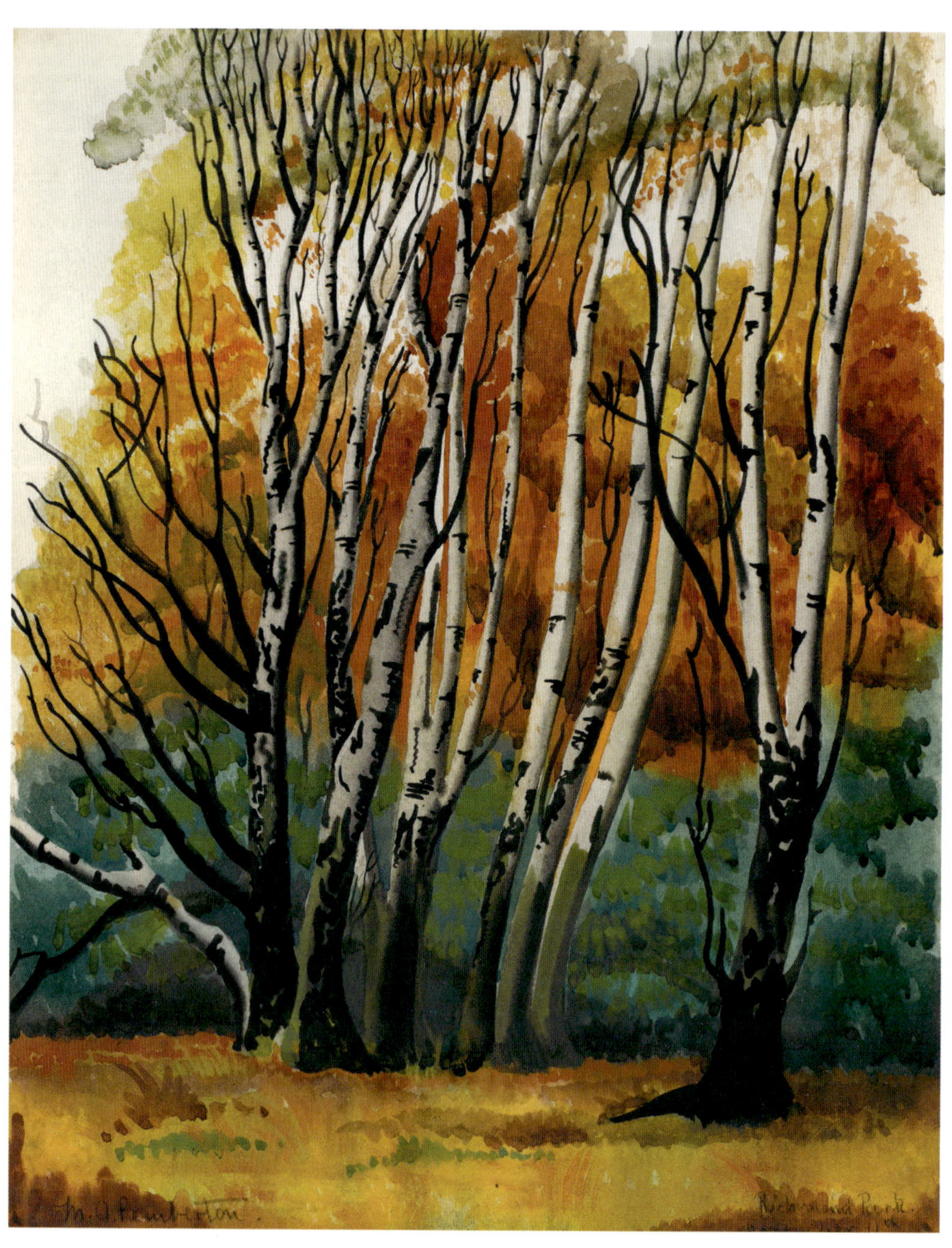

Birch trees – Richmond Park, c.1930, signed, inscribed 'Richmond Park November 11th',
watercolour on paper, 21 × 14 ½ in. (53.5 × 35.5 cm).

Little of Muriel Pemberton's early work is known to have survived — these two watercolours can be dated to the early 1930s. Canal boats (known as Butties), of the type depicted, were horse drawn and would have been later converted to motor boats after the mid 30s.

As a Londoner, Pemberton would have frequented Richmond Park — the setting for *Birch Trees* — a favourite haunt of artists to paint *en plein air*. Easily portable and fast drying, watercolour lent itself to painting on the spot and was as a result an adept medium for capturing atmospheric affects. However, unlike drawing or oil painting, watercolour could not be corrected and therefore required a surety of intention.

As a student at The Royal College of Art, Pemberton was awarded the first ever Diploma in Fashion by the College, in 1931. Her fellow student and fianceé, Stanley Lewis, recalled being berated by Pemberton for not being more modern in his approach. Pemberton went on to pioneer art-school training in fashion in Britain (at St Martin's School of Art), influencing attitudes to design throughout Europe.

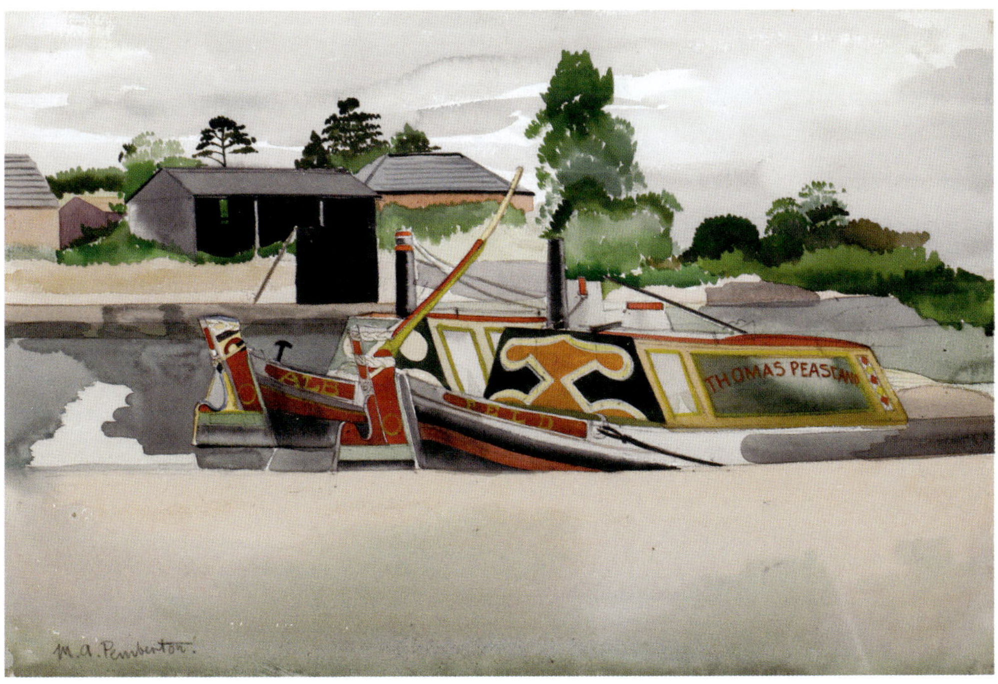

Butties, early 1930s, signed, inscribed '2',
watercolour on paper, 14 ½ × 21 in. (35.5 × 53.5 cm).

Lucy Kemp-Welch (1869-1958)

Lucy Kemp-Welch specialised in depicting working horses. In this study, she has expertly but sparsely sketched in the figure of the horse handler, while emphasising the horses with colour and detail. The animals' muscles, delicate noses, and soft hair demand the viewer's full attention. The realistic detail reflects Kemp-Welch's thorough knowledge of animal anatomy gained during her studies at a horse hospital in Christchurch, Dorset. She later applied this knowledge when travelling with John Sanger's circus from 1926.

Kemp-Welch first became interested in horses as artistic subject matter when, during her childhood in Bournemouth, she was encouraged to sketch ponies in the New Forest. She was later elected one of the first two female members of the Royal Society of British Artists in England. Her talent at depicting animals was also recognised when she was awarded medals at the Paris Salon.

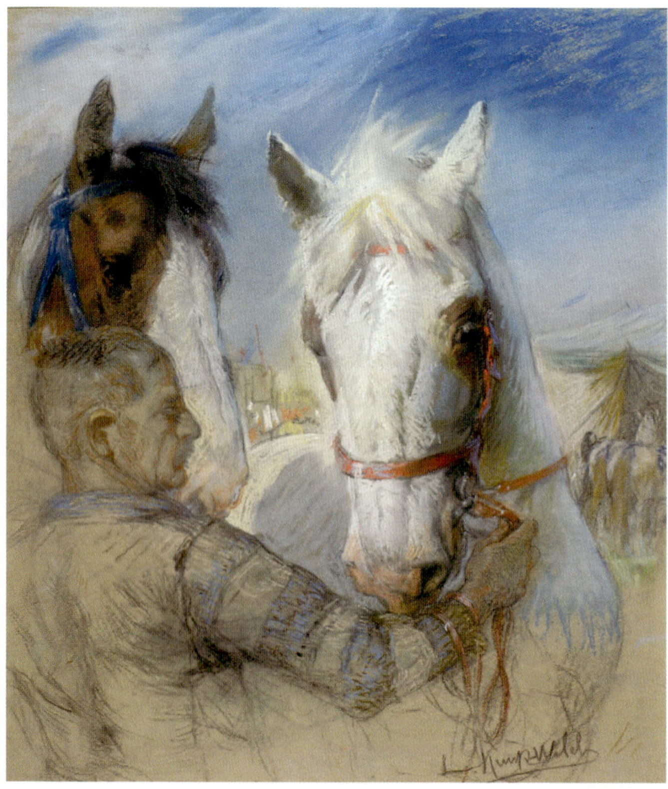

Circus Man Holding Two Horses, after 1926, signed, pastel on paper, 16 ¼ x 13¾ in. (41.3 x 34.8 cm). Bequeathed by Arthur J Fenwick 1963.

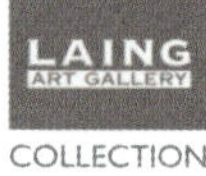

COLLECTION

Frances Hodgkins (1869-1947)

Frances Hodgkins sought to achieve a balance in her pictures between likeness and abstract qualities of colour and form. This is evident in the bold blue and brown outlines of the boy's face in this picture. Colours are blurred together or show through later layers of paint. The effect is to create a rich surface, though the colours themselves are fairly subdued.

Although originally from New Zealand, Hodgkins spent much of her life in Europe. She lived for several years in France, where she saw art by Henri Matisse and was impressed by the flowing line and sensuous colour of his early figure paintings. Her talents were recognised in Paris when she became one of the first women to teach watercolour painting at the prestigious Académie Colarossi. She also exhibited many times at the Royal Academy of Arts in London. In 1929, Hodgkins joined the avant-garde 7&5 group of artists based in St Ives, Cornwall.

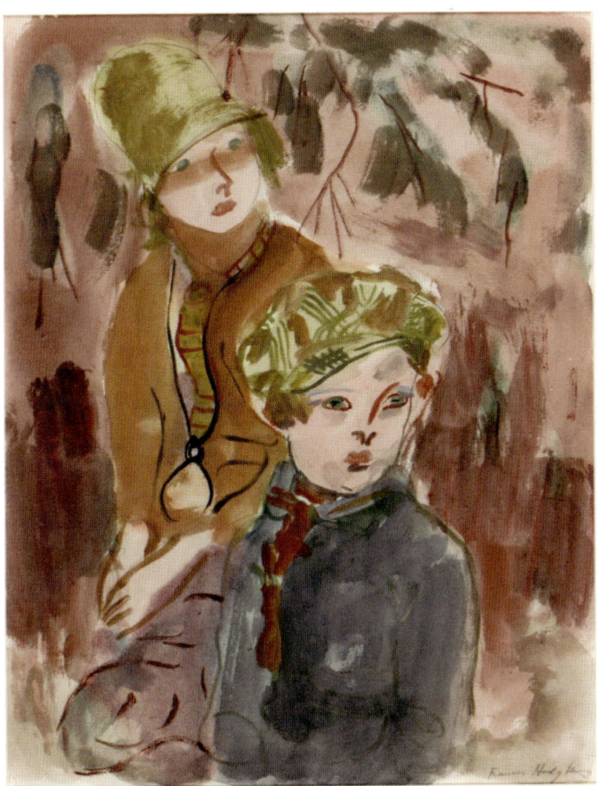

Boy and Girl, c.1930, signed,
gouache and watercolour on paper (on board),
18 ¼ × 21 in. (46.7 × 53.4 cm). Purchased 1931.

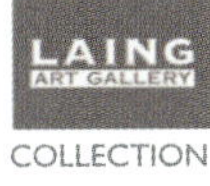

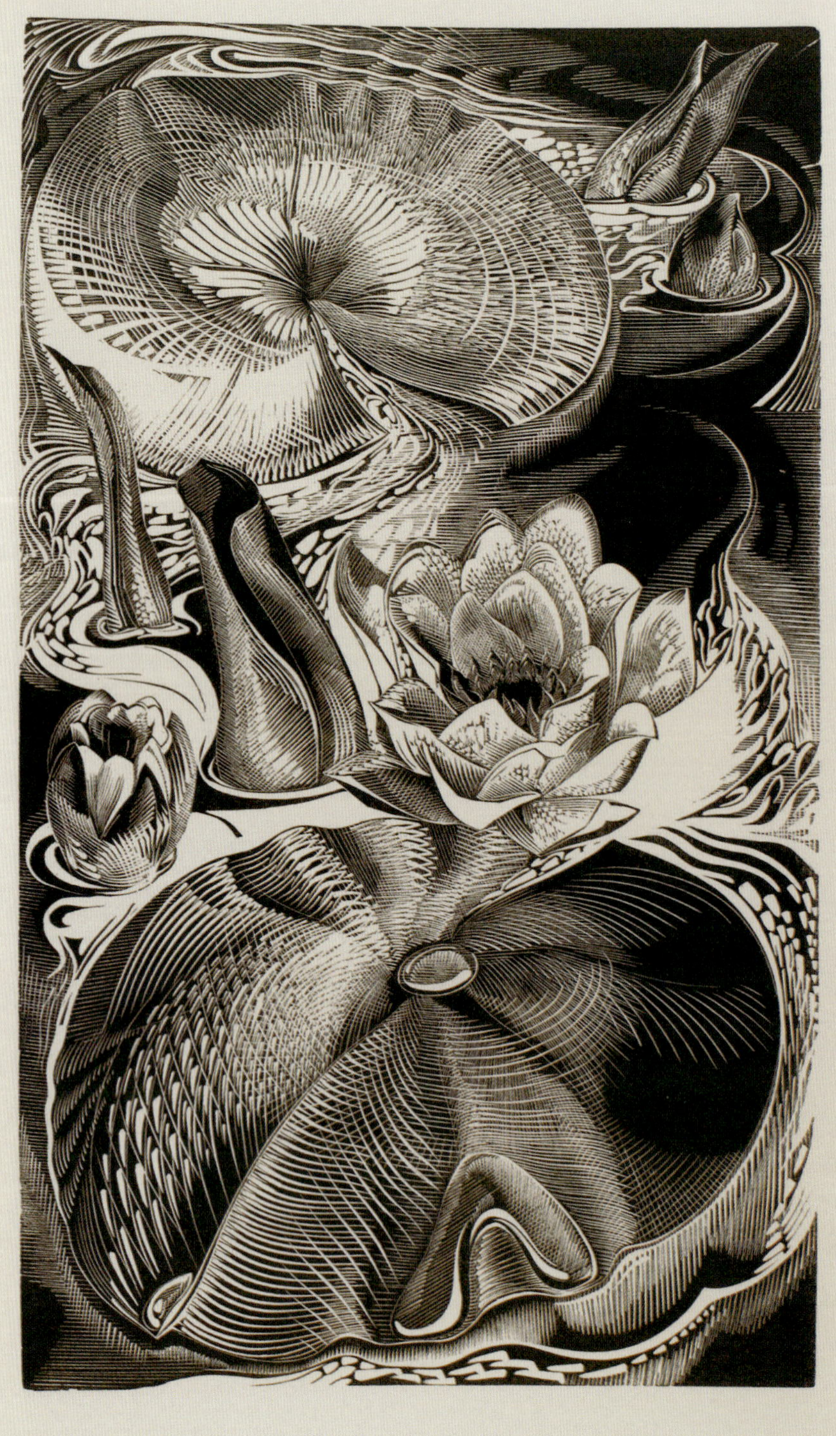

Gertrude Hermes (1901-1983)

In his book *A History of Wood Engraving* (1978), Albert Garrett, the President of the Society of Wood Engravers, described how in *Water Lilies*, Gertrude Hermes 'had solved in her own terms the language for engraving a large circular plane that has gentle undulations. For most people, a waterlily leaf is a solid plane but in the engraving Hermes sees it as a space plane solution'. Hermes, who was one of the most imaginative and innovative wood engravers of her generation, drew much of her inspiration from nature. Trained by Leon Underwood at his art school in Hammersmith, she captured all manner of natural forms observed from the world around her – plants, animals, insects – with a rapidly flowing line. Transferring her preliminary sketches onto blocks of fine-grained wood, her distinctive style combined great technical skill with a bold sense of design. Described by the novelist Naomi Mitchison as a 'a magician – or if you like priestess', Hermes' unique achievement lay in the way she rendered nature as dynamic and living, the feeling of movement giving the engravings an almost three-dimensional quality. 'By the end of the second world war', Garrett wrote, 'Hermes in engraving is what [Barbara] Hepworth is in sculpture'.

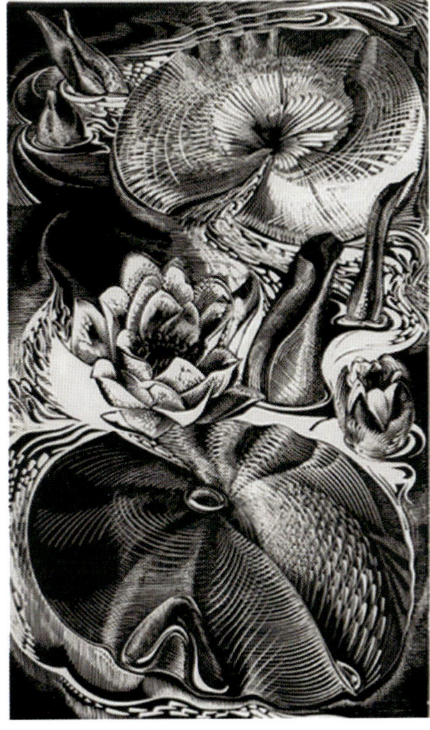

Water Lilies, 1930,
original woodblock, 9 × 5 in. (23 × 13.1 cm).

Water Lilies,
wood engraving on paper, image size: 9 × 5 in. (23 × 13.1 cm).
Printed posthumously from the block. The original wood engraving was printed in 1930 in an edition of 30.

Mary Adshead (1904-1995)

The format of *Livestock Market (recto)* and *Picking Tea Leaves* (verso), suggests that both designs may have been part of an intended mural scheme. *The Gong*, created for an unpublished book of poems by Anne Harding Thompson, is accompanied by a verse which starts with the lines: 'This crazy old woman is singing a song, and beating like mad on her old brass gong'. All three works demonstrate Mary Adshead's preference for simplified colours and shapes, and a delight in humourous narrative which she combined with a hint of neo-Victorianism.

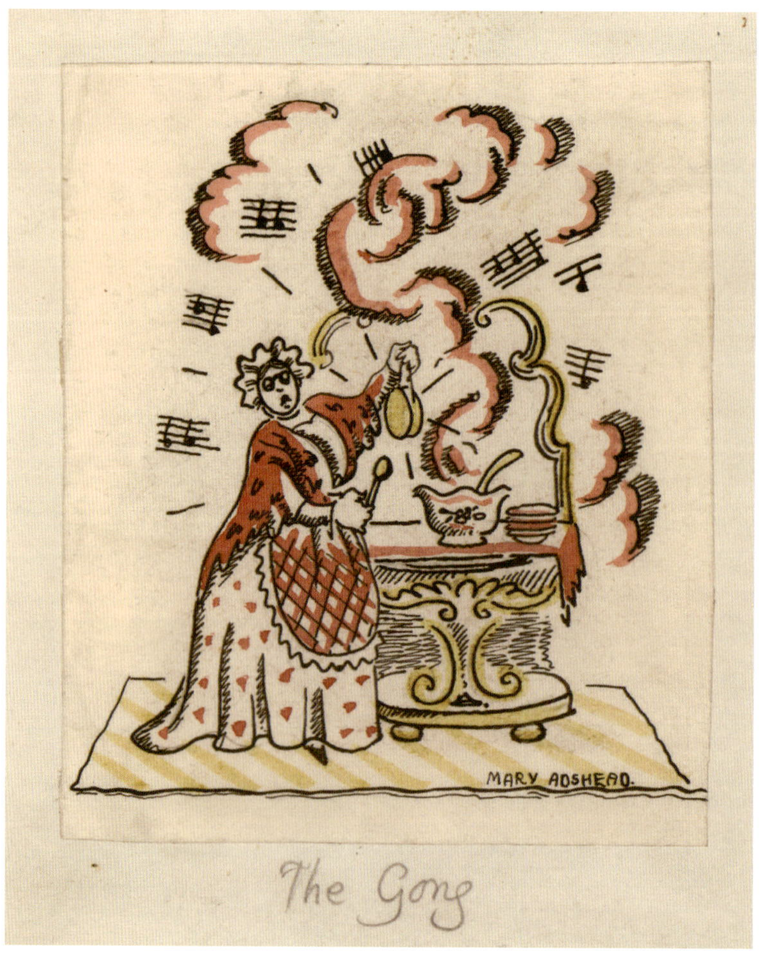

The Gong, signed and titled,
pen & ink and watercolour on paper, 6 ¾ x 7 ½ in. (17.2 x 19 cm).

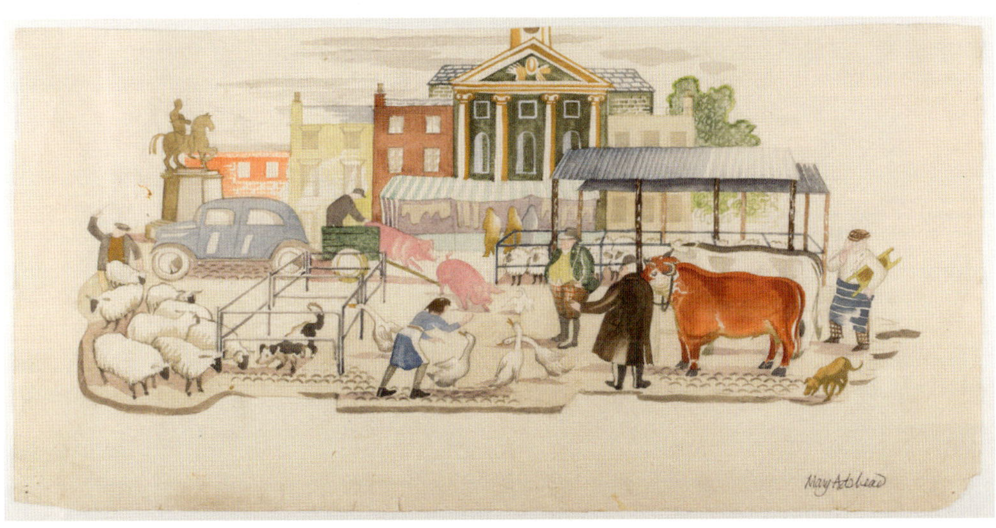

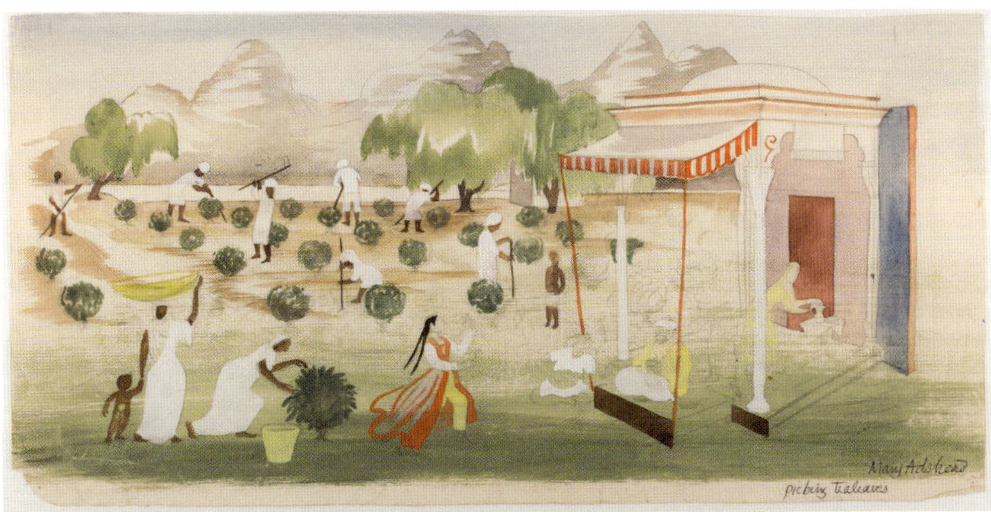

Livestock Market (recto) and *Picking Tealeaves* (verso), c.1930, signed in pen, gouache on paper, 10 × 20 in. (25.3 × 50.8 cm).

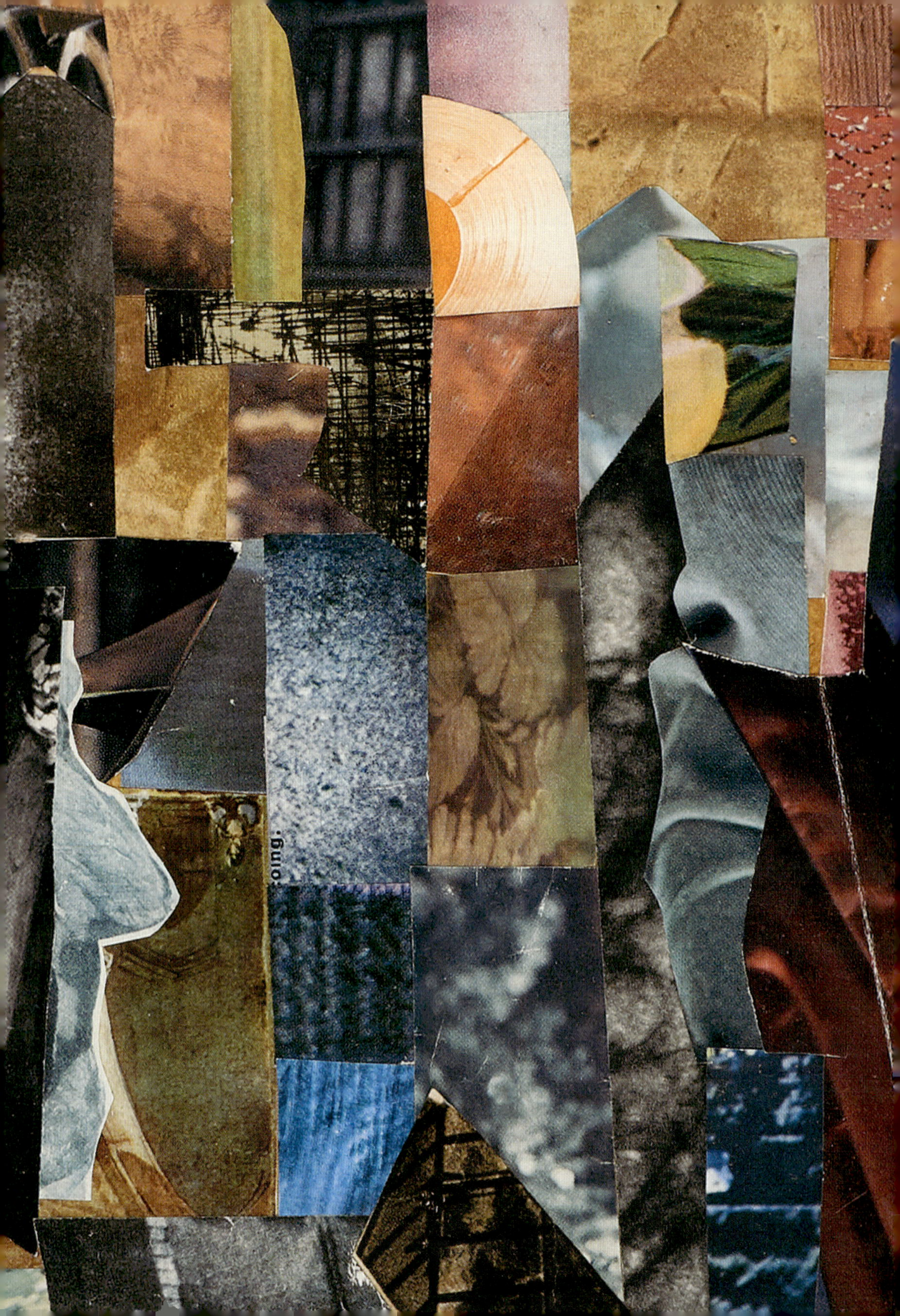
oing.

Praising Valentine Dobrée's collages in an exhibition of her work at the Claridge Gallery, London, in 1931, a critic for *The Sketch* observed, 'her pictures might also have been called mosaics, as they are made out of different coloured wall-paper cut out and pasted together to form Vorticist designs…Her medium does not, as a rule, admit of brilliance, and I found the subdued tones of her patchwork pictures lovely.'

In *The Event*, Dobrée uses a triptych format to frame an almost cinematic juxtaposition of wallpaper, marbled paper, photographs and journal cuttings, which overlap to create multiple viewpoints, a technique that places her in active dialogue with cubist collage artists, such as Pablo Picasso (1881-1973) and Juan Gris (1887-1927). The defamiliarization generated by the rearrangement of elements on the paper, including images of modern buildings, sea and sky, and unidentified objects, also creates multiple realities found in surrealist collage. For Dobrée, collage offered a means of fixing attention on the fragmentation of modern society. 'The fragments lie around us', she wrote in 1963, '…haunted by experience, extending into a half-conscious dream world'.

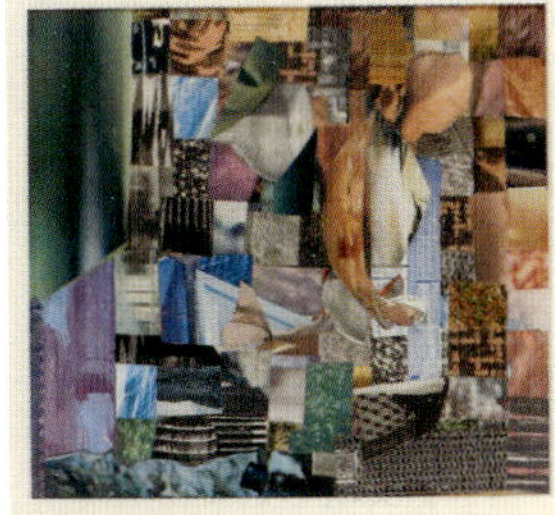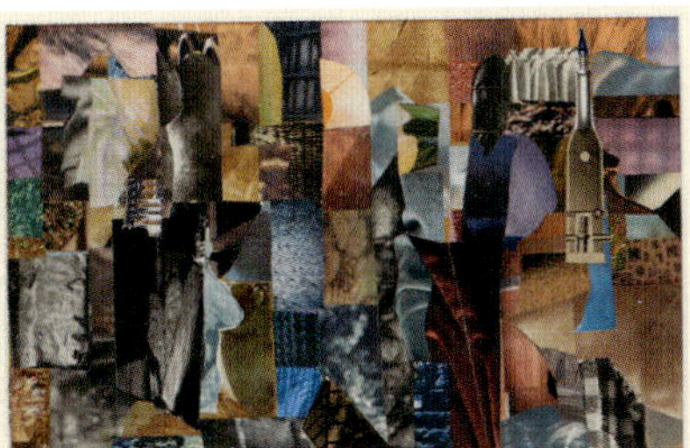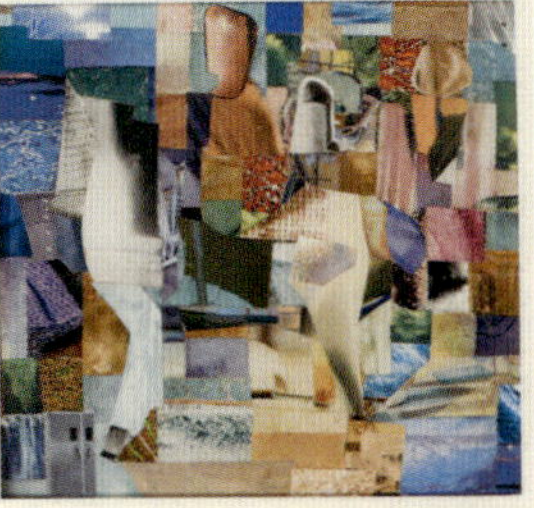

The Event, (triptych), early 1960s, signed and titled on a label to the reverse,
collage on card, left and right panels: 7 ¼ × 7 ½ in. (18.5 × 19.5 cm), central panel: 7 ¼ × 11 ½ in. (18.5 × 29 cm).

Edith Granger-Taylor (1887-1958)

Having learnt pastel from Henry Tonks whilst attending the Slade in 1919, Edith Granger-Taylor worked almost exclusively in this medium, or crayon, for the rest of her life.

Reporting on her 1932 exhibition at the Beaux Arts Gallery, London, the art critic from *The Scotsman* wrote that Granger-Taylor used pastel with 'extraordinary facility and intelligence, and designs with grace. She has a style personal and fluent (…), full of pleasant flourishes and tricks of technique'. The writer goes on to praise the tone and shape of Granger-Taylor's near-abstract style, saying that the 'peculiar sweetness (of pastel) proves fatal to all but draughtsmen with a strong and healthy colour sense'.

In spite of such critical reception, her increasing frustration as a female artist working in the inter-war years, expressed in paintings such as *Allegory* (1934) (which she referred to as a "delicate feminist satire") caused Granger-Taylor to retreat from the art world, and after the 1930s her work would not be exhibited again in her lifetime. Her remarkable abstract compositions date to the 1930s.

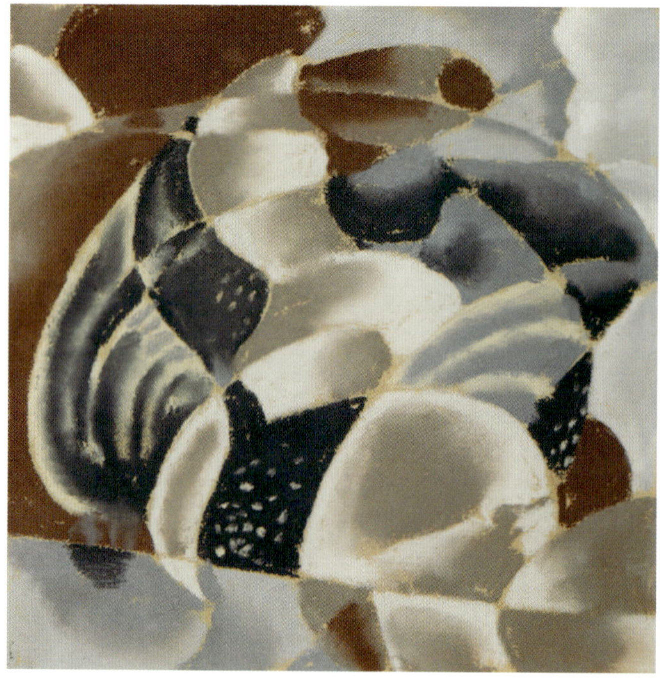

Small Grey Abstract, c.1934,
pastel on paper, 6 ¾ x 6 ¾ in. (17.15 x 17.15 cm).

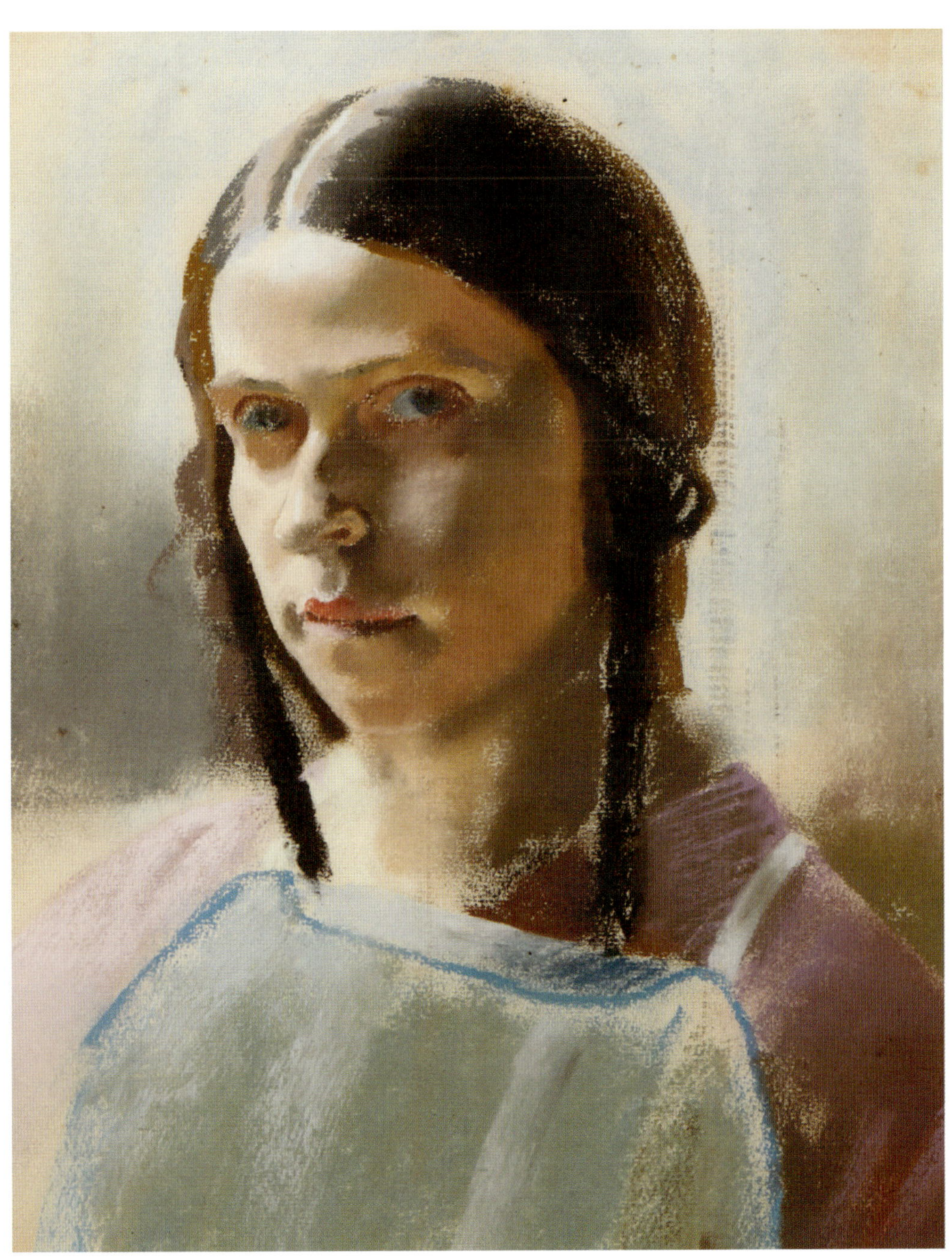

Self-portrait, c.1920,
pastel on paper, 13 ¼ × 10 ¼ in. (34 × 26 cm).

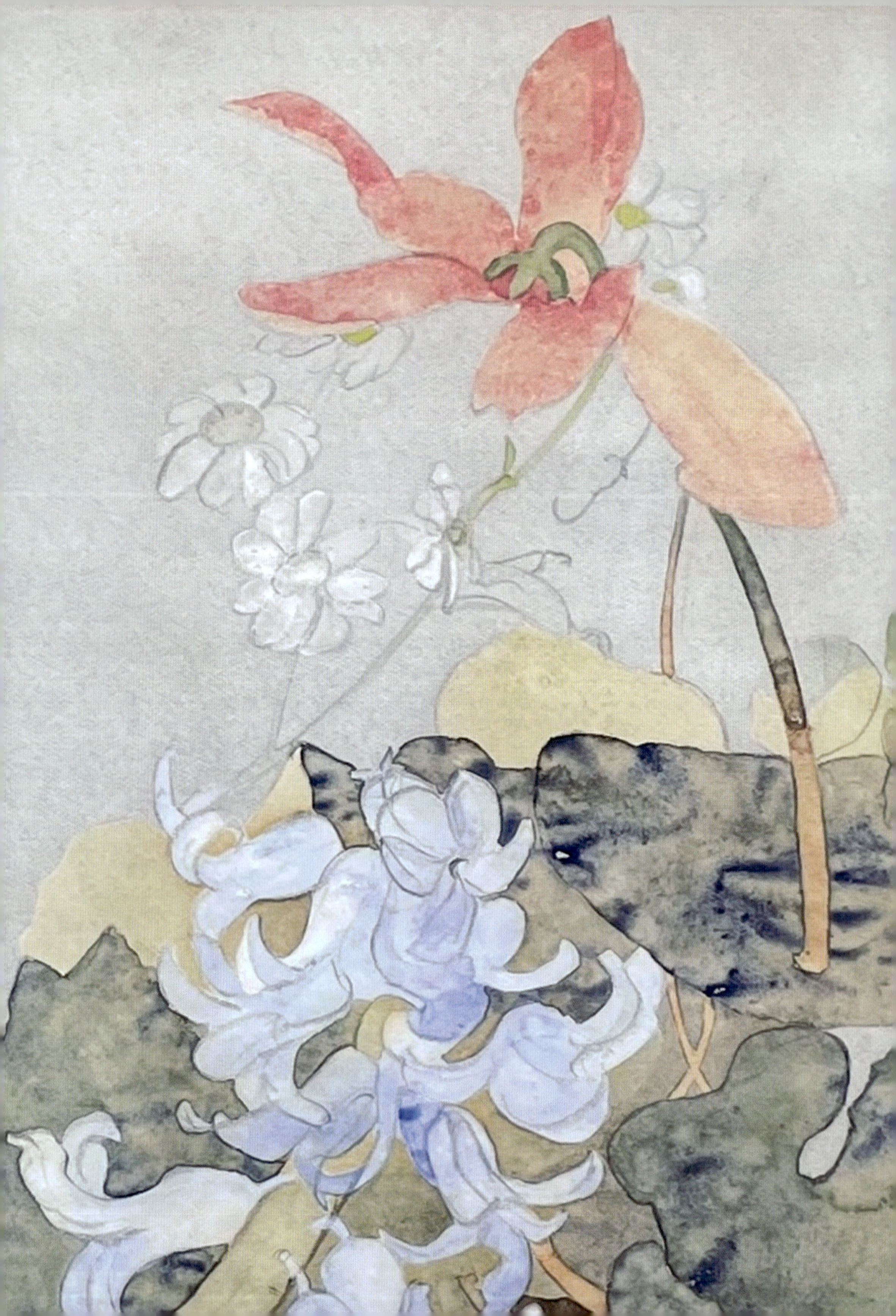

This early watercolour by Ithell Colquhoun precedes her first solo exhibition of *Exotic Plant Decorations* at the Fine Art Society in 1936. Amy Hale has noted that it is through these detailed botanical studies that one can trace her stylistic slide into Surrealism. Indeed, Colquhoun herself remarked that the influence of Dali and Surrealism prophetically 'took root' in these studies, for while she was in Paris as early as 1931, the movement would not truly resonate until after she had attended the London International Surrealism Exhibition at the New Burlington Galleries in June, 1936.

Flowers were a recurring subject of Colquhoun's art. They are often painted in a crisp, technical manner, while likely imbued with some symbolic hidden meaning, given Colquhoun's interest in Occultism and esoteric theories. According to Michel Remy, these early flower paintings not only indicate Colquhoun's fascination for elaborate shapes, but 'hint at the fantastical worlds inaccessible to rational man.'

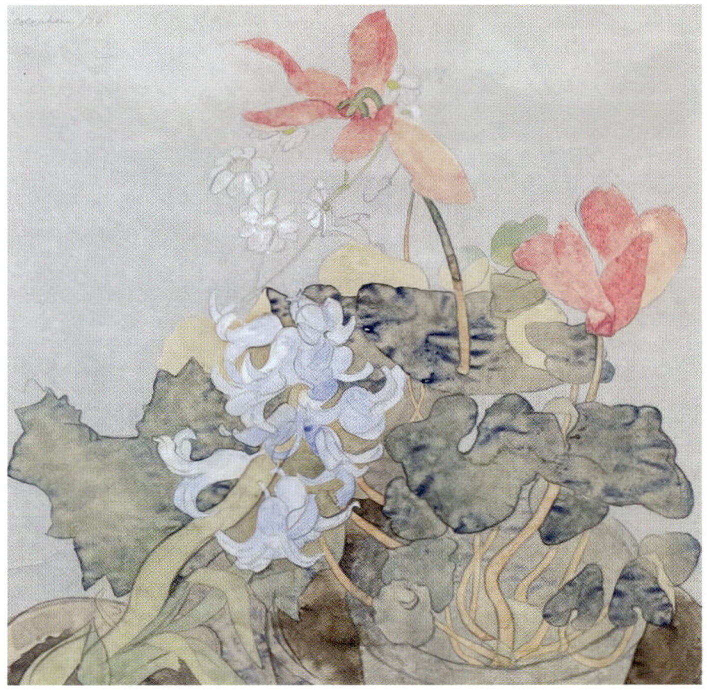

Hyacinth and Cyclamen, 1934, signed and dated,
watercolour on paper, 10 x 10 ½ (25.4 x 25.9 cm).

Vanessa Bell (1879-1961)

This work was described as a design for a ceramic tile when it was first exhibited at the Folio Fine Art Ltd., London, in 1967. It was likely produced for the potter, Phyllis Keyes, whom Vanessa Bell met in 1931. Keyes had a workshop in Warren Street, and supplied Bell and Duncan Grant with a variety of tiles, pots, jugs and vases, either thrown by her or cast from designs that the artists provided. These ceramics then often featured in decorative schemes completed by the Bloomsbury artists.

The simplicity of this tile design reduces the artist's style almost to its essence. Robert Travers observes that while Bell's oil paintings after the end of the First World War 'became increasingly built-up, saturated and developed, her decorative work inherited the freedom of line, colour and abstract composition which she pursued so fruitfully between 1910 and 1918'.

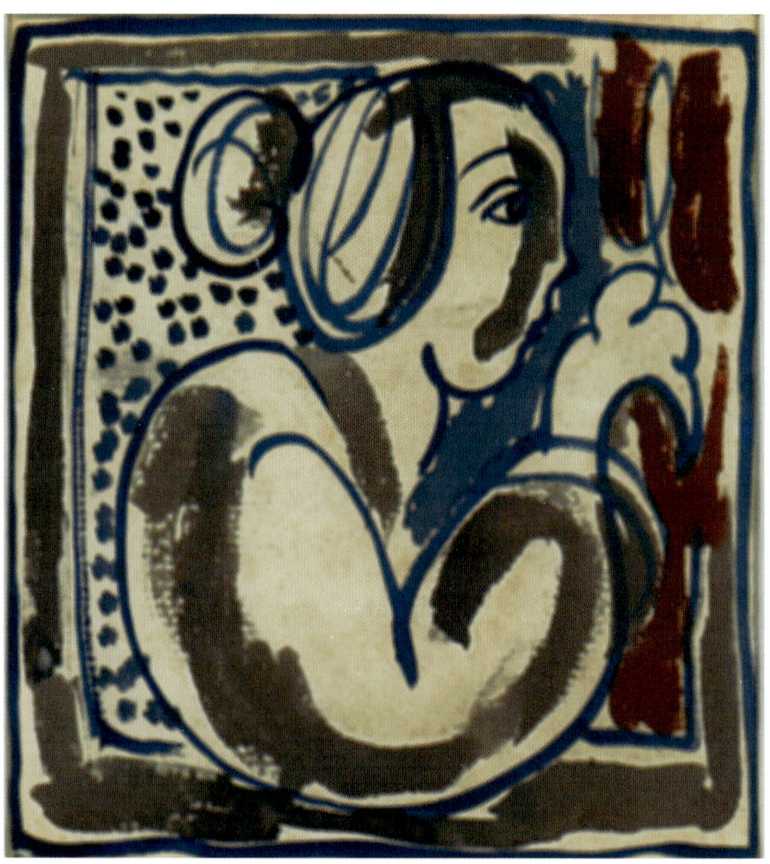

Portrait of a Girl in Profile, with a Decorated Background,
gouache on paper, 5 ½ x 5 ½ in. (14 x 14 cm).

Catherine Dawson Giles (1878-1955)

Catherine Giles exhibited with the Roman Catholic Guild of Artists alongside Glyn Philpot and Eric Gill in the 1930s. This composition was presented by Giles to Gertrude Rachel Levy (1883-1966) who commissioned a similar work in tempera for Seaford Church in 1936. Levy was a British author and cultural historian who wrote about comparative mythology, matriarchy, epic poetry and archaeology. Using the faintest of outlines in pencil, the composition is constructed in bold, flat planes of gouache. The ground of the buff coloured paper is left bare in parts to create areas of flesh colour and folds in the drapery, as well as the form of the landscape behind.

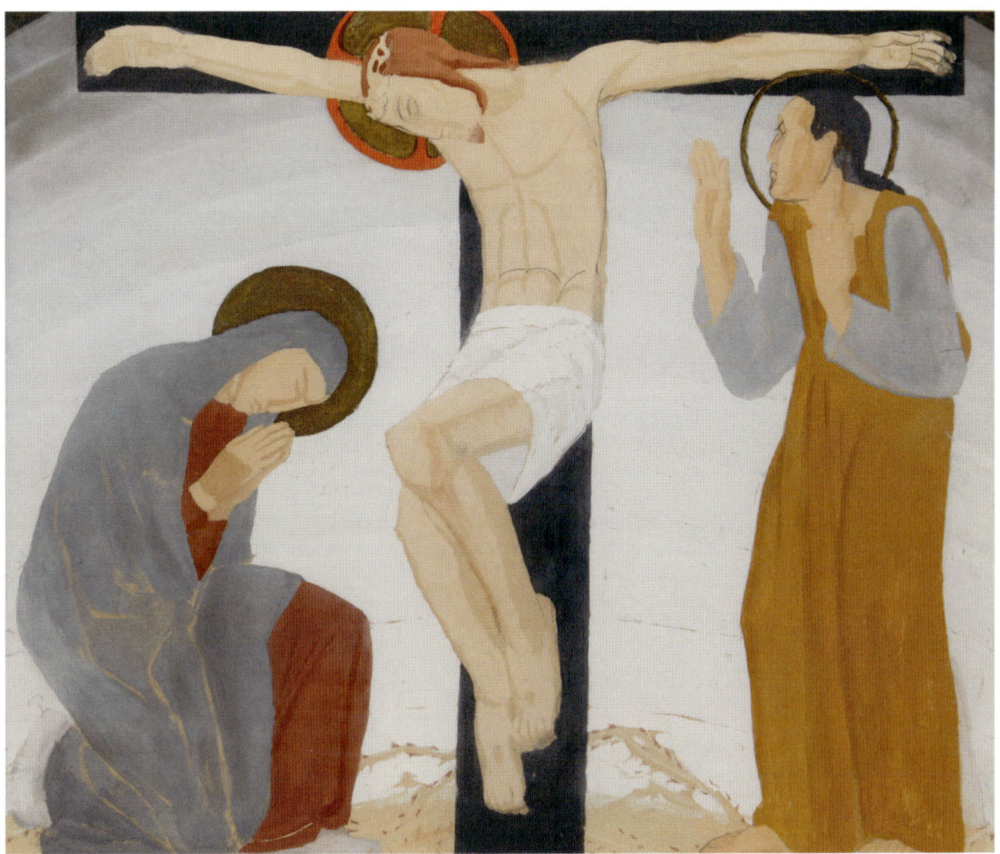

Crucifixion, 1936,
gouache on paper, 23 × 26 ¾ in. (58.4 × 67.9 cm).

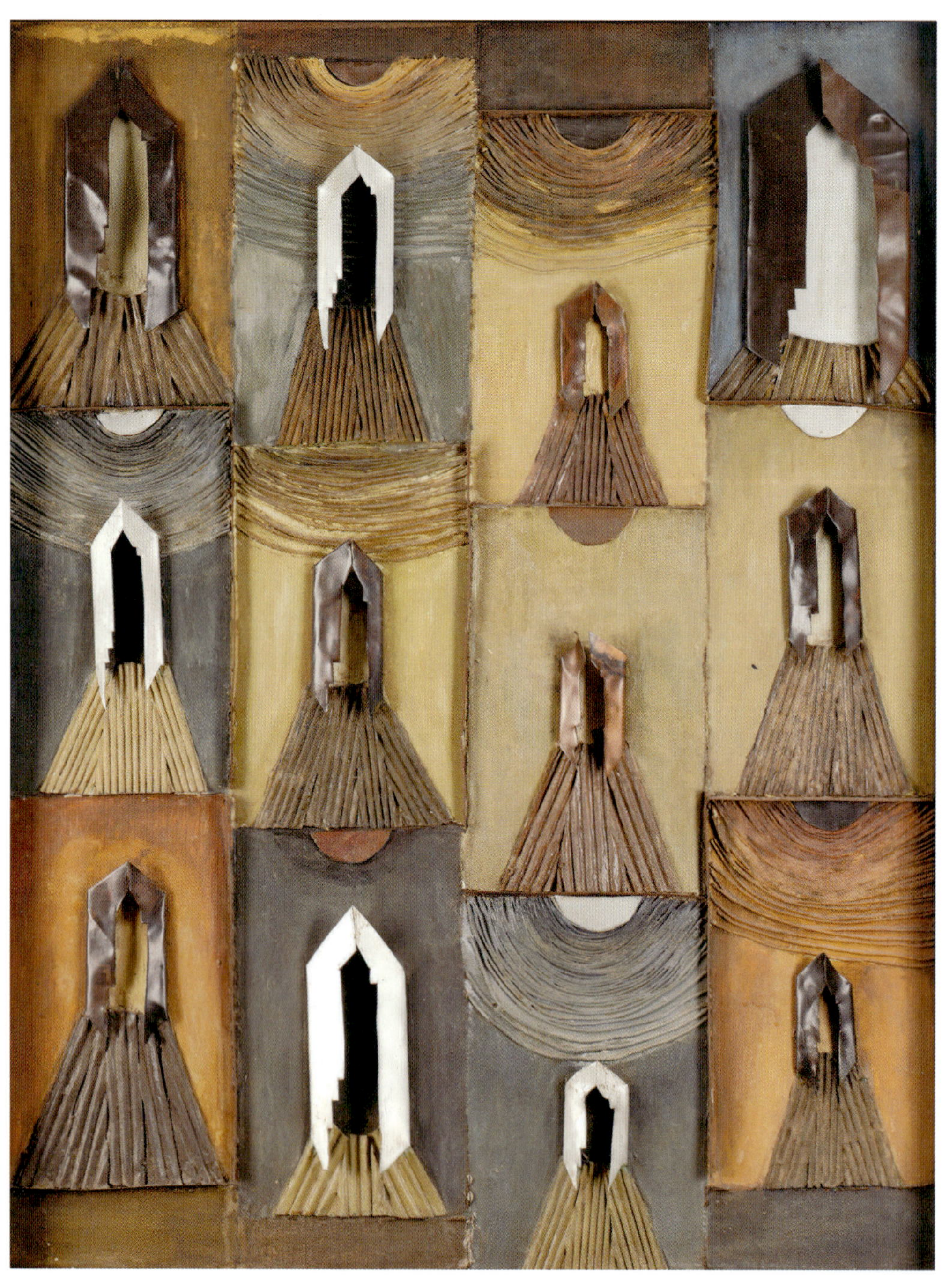

Towers and Helmets, 1960s,
mixed media including corrugated cardboard, sheet metal and string on board, 36 x 27 ½ in. (91.5 x 70 cm).

As Rachel Reckitt's style evolved, her interest in three-dimensional form became evident. The figures in her paintings and drawings were composed of planes resembling cubes and cones, almost as if they were studies for the works she was later to realise in sculpture. From the 1960s onwards, Reckitt all but abandoned painting and engraving to concentrate on boxed constructions, collages in mixed-media set within wooden frames. Deeply inspired by the teachings of Harry Horrobin, a former armourer, whose courses on metalwork she attended, Reckitt constructed collages using soft metal and painted corrugated cardboard. *Towers and Helmets*, on which corrugated cardboard, string and sheet copper is applied to an aluminium base, is typical of her highly creative three-dimension compositions in which a motif is repeated across a linear plane. Although in the 1930s she had made a number of mixed-media signs for pubs in Exmoor, their utilitarian function was far removed from the spiritual aspirations of these later works.

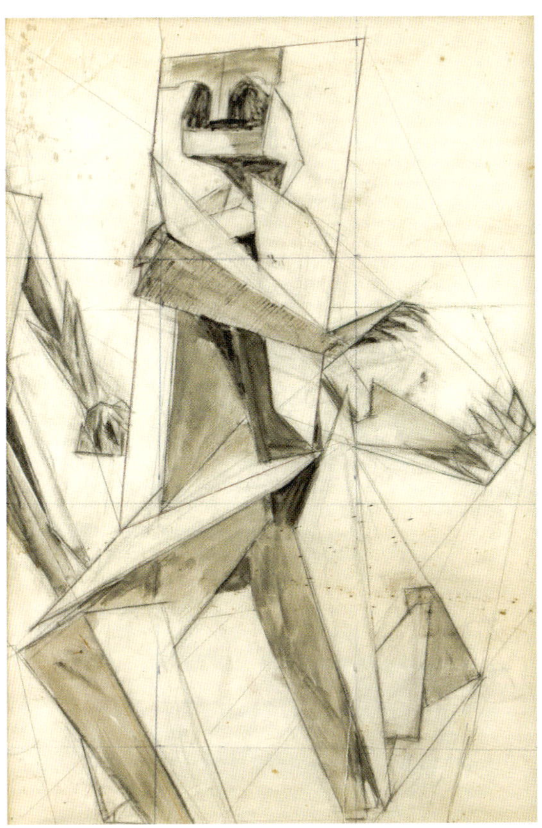

Cubist Figure, 1950s,
pencil, pen & ink and wash on paper, squared,
29 ½ x 19 ½ in. (75 x 49.8 cm).

Gladys Hynes (1888-1958)

Although fifteen years separate *The Railway Carriage* and *Siamese Cat*, Gladys Hynes' interest in a Vorticist-inflected aesthetic – jagged, rhythmical and linear – which she first embraced in 1919, energizes both works. Before the First World War, Hynes had been part of a thriving second-generation of Newlyn painters, along with Laura Knight and Dod Procter, producing a striking body of work inspired by Cornwall's pools and rocks, cliff tops and ocean views. In 1919 she moved to London, taking lodgings in South Hampstead with the poet John Rodker, whose Ovid press was publishing graphic work by former members of the Vorticist group. In 1927, Hynes received what was to be the most important commission of her career, to illustrate a folio edition of Ezra Pound's *Cantos 17–27*, published by Rodker. Under this influence, and revelling in her new independence as an observer of the urban scene, Hynes' pictures evolved noticeably towards a more modern aesthetic and subject-matter, a stylistic change that affronted the *Daily Mail's* critic, who in 1922 lamented that she 'has turned away from all that is beautiful and soulful'.

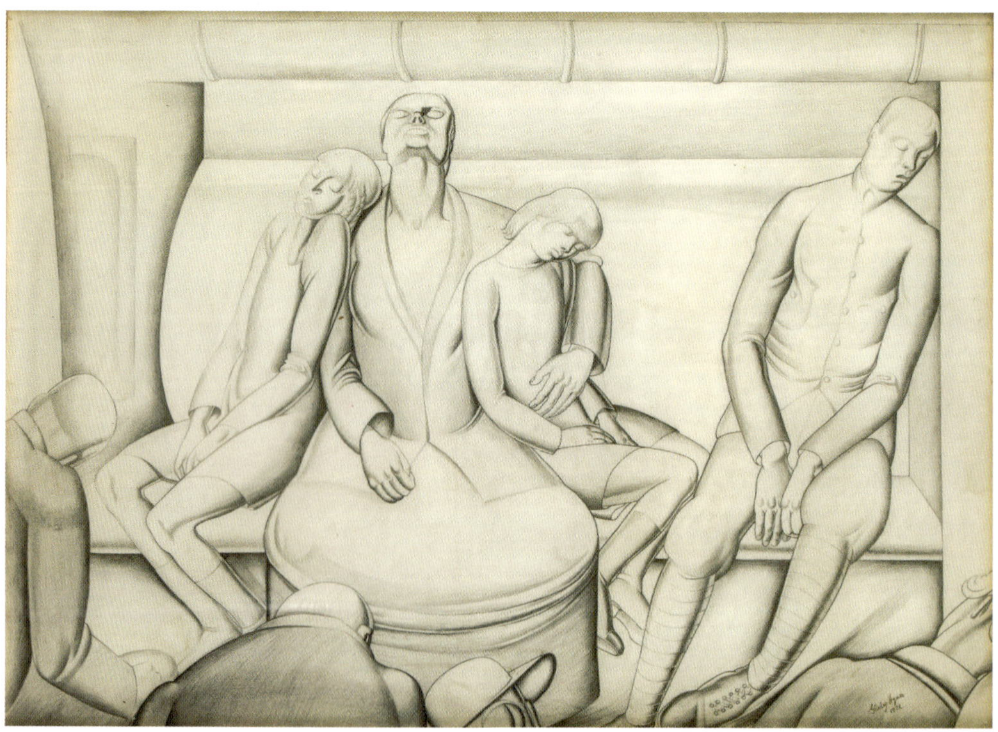

The Railway Carriage, 1922, signed and dated,
pencil on paper, 22 x 30 in. (56 x 76.2 cm).

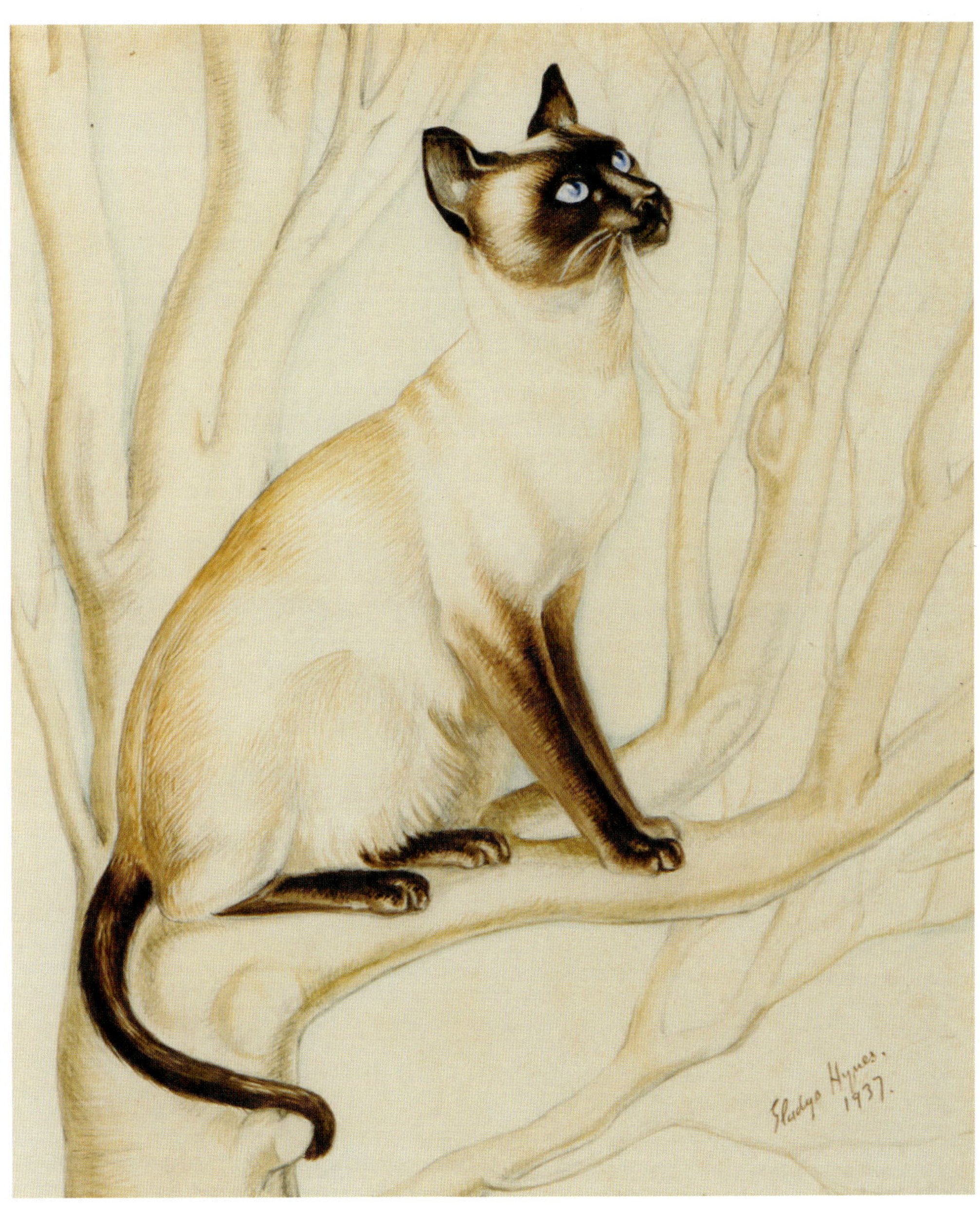

Siamese Cat in a Tree, 1937, signed and dated,
watercolour and crayon on paper, 11 ½ × 8 ¾ in. (29 × 22.5 cm).

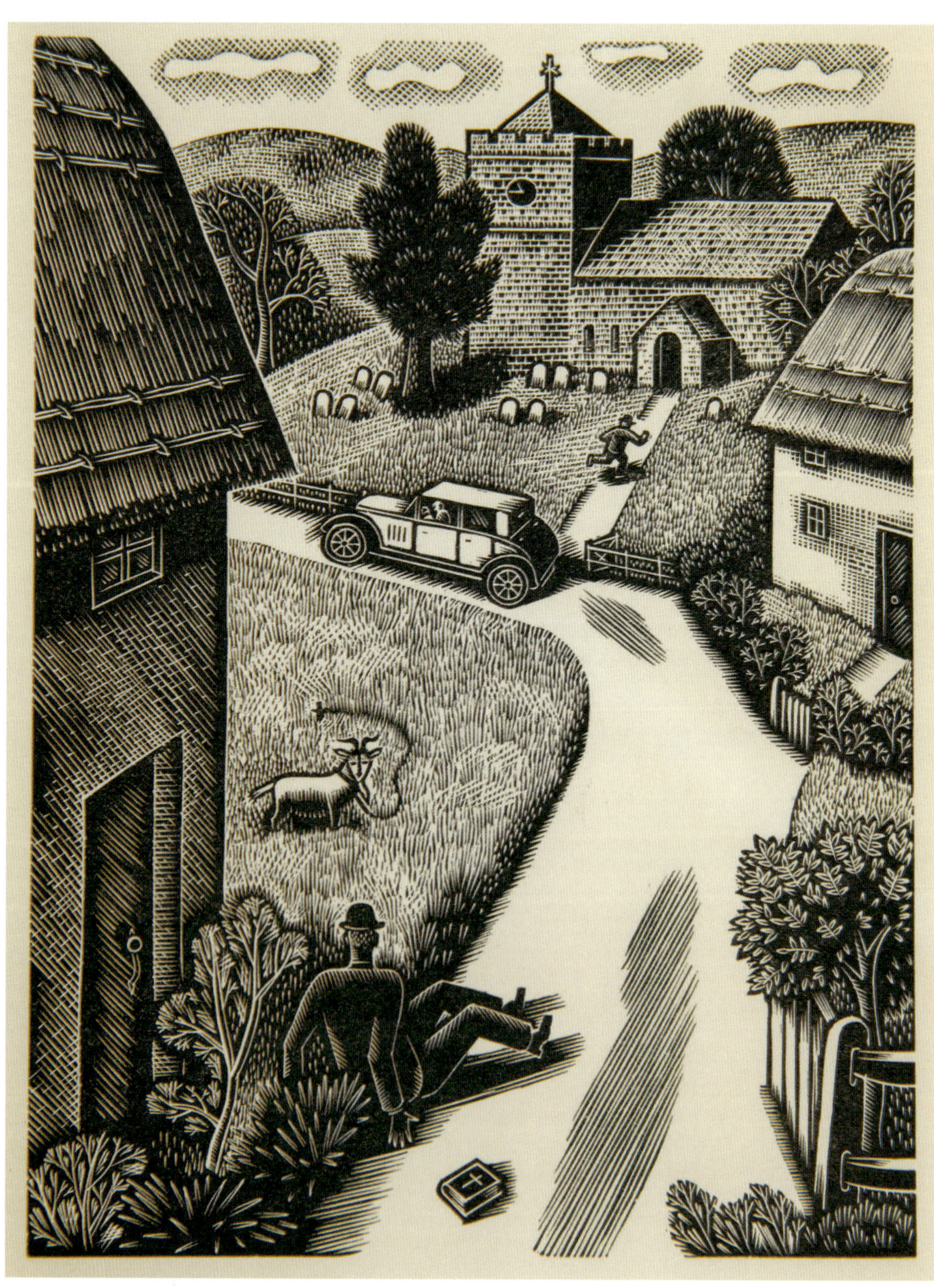

The Rev. Humble Arrives at Church, 1937,
wood engraving on paper, 5 ½ x 4 ¾ in. (14.2 x 12 cm).
Printed from the original block by The Golden Cockerel Press in *Goat Green* by T.F. Powys, 1937.

Apple Picking was printed from the original block by the Whittington Press, in 1985, having been first issued in 1952. *The Rev. Humble* was created for the 1937 edition of *Goat Green* by T F Powys, printed by the Golden Cockerel Press.

After studying at Goldsmiths' College of Art in London, from 1930 Morgan attended the Grosvenor School of Modern Art, London, where she was taught and strongly influenced by Iain Macnab. The Grosvenor School was a progressive art school, and the championing of wood engraving and linocuts fitted with its democratic approach to the arts. The main body of her work drew upon the landscape and buildings around Petworth, where she lived all her life, and the neighbouring South Downs. Her work was also inspired by Douglas Percy Bliss, Eric Ravilious, and Tirzah Garwood.

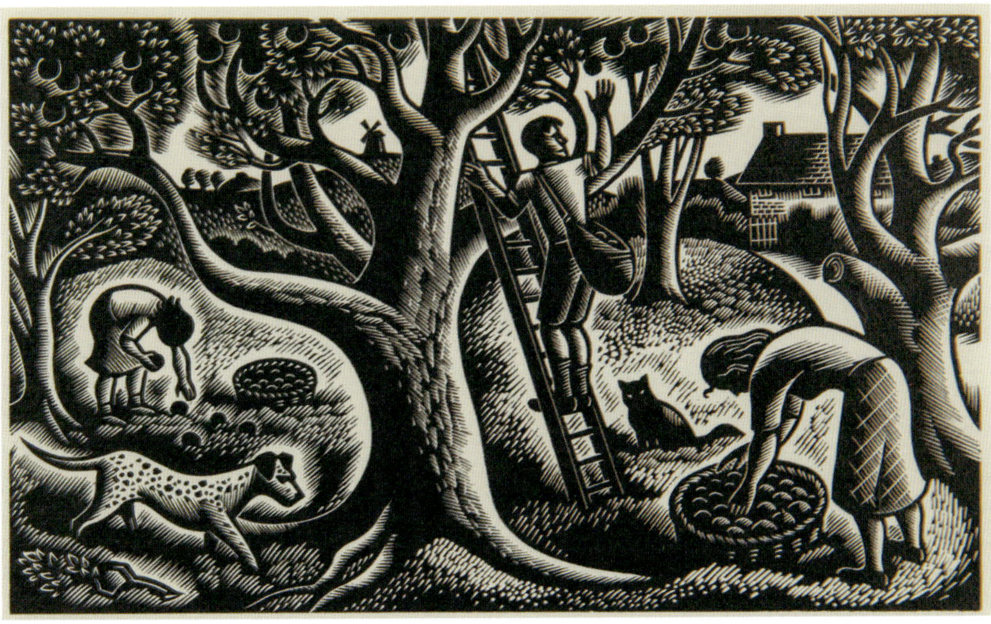

Apple Picking, 1952,
wood engraving on paper, 5 ½ × 4 ¾ in. (9.8 × 16 cm).
Printed from the original block by the Whittington Press in 1985.

Margaret Duncan (1906-1979)

Little is known about Margaret Duncan, other than that during the 1930s and 40s she worked as an art teacher at Huyton College, Liverpool, where she amused staff and pupils with 'light-hearted drawings – quite good enough for *Punch* – in which she perpetuated certain phrases or episodes' of the comings and goings of life at the school. In the preliminary sketch for *Reigate and its Environments*, which is inscribed 'Design for Mural Decoration', Duncan has taken her view from the tower of St Mary's Church with the North Downs forming a backdrop. Squared-up and rendered in watercolour, pen and ink, the sketch is evidence of the thought and care that went into the planning of the 'mural'. The surviving finished four-panelled screen, painted in egg tempera, faithfully follows the preliminary sketch but is populated with characters partaking in a variety of country pursuits.

Similar figures can be seen in the study 'Jean von Bloch', (also possibly a design for a larger painting). Here Duncan paints a vignette of a family on a stroll, with a little boy, a woman and a man (possibly a depiction of the playwright Jean-Richard Bloch) fancifully attired in historical costume. Both works demonstrate Duncan's talent for extracting the underlying geometry of landscape and figures to form a coherent rhythmic whole.

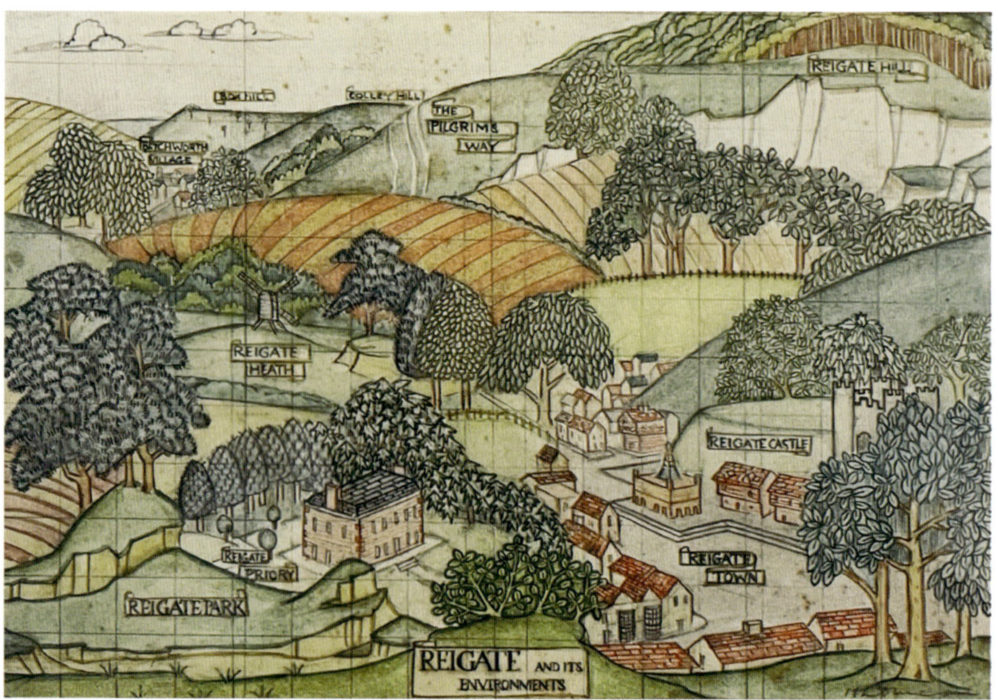

Reigate and its Environments 'design for mural decoration',
signed and inscribed with title on the mount, late 1930s,
watercolour over pen and ink on paper, squared, 6 × 10 in (15.5 × 25.5 cm).

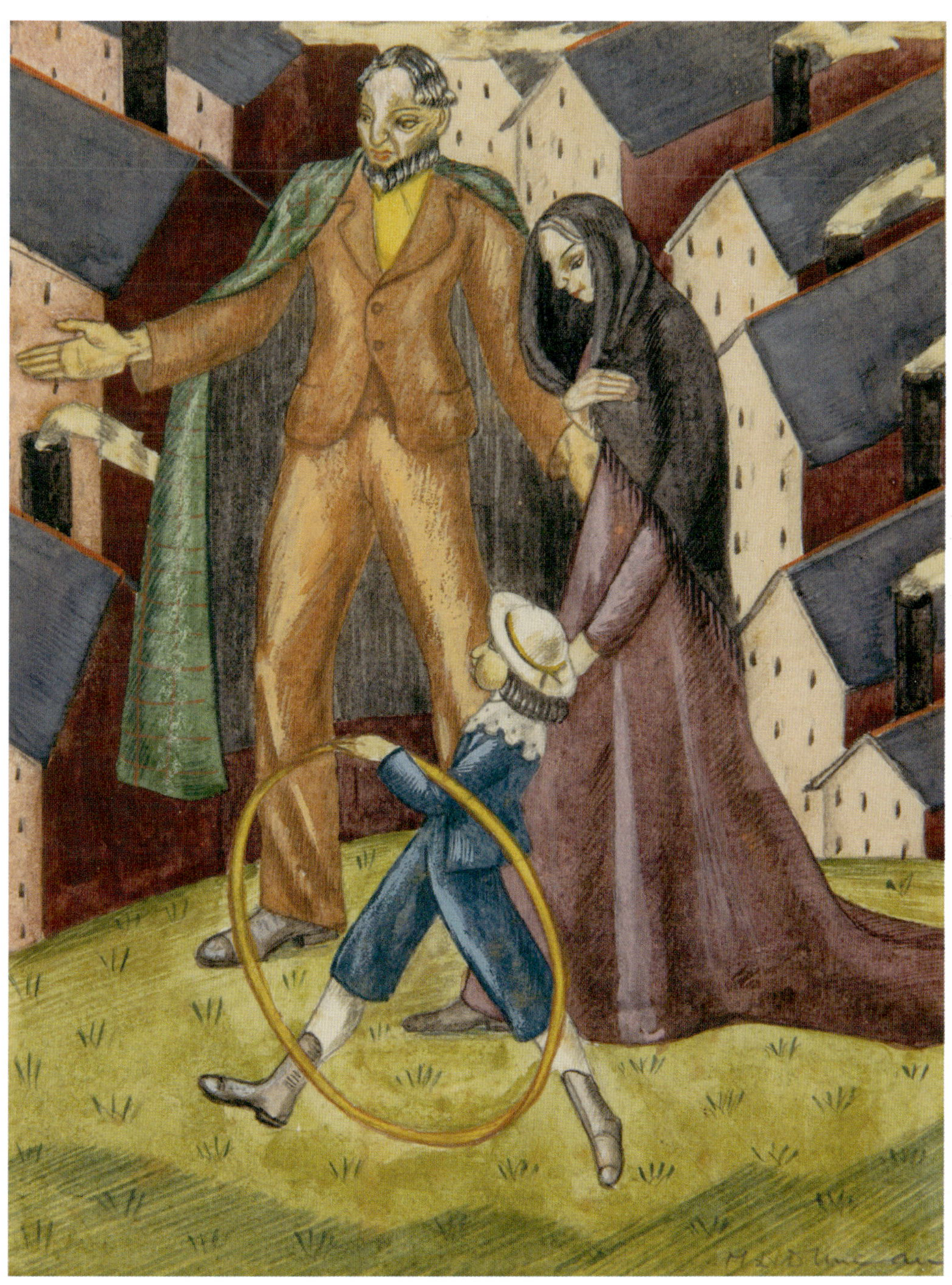

Jean von Bloch, late 1920s,
pencil and watercolour on paper, 6 ¼ × 4 ¾ in. (16 × 12 cm).

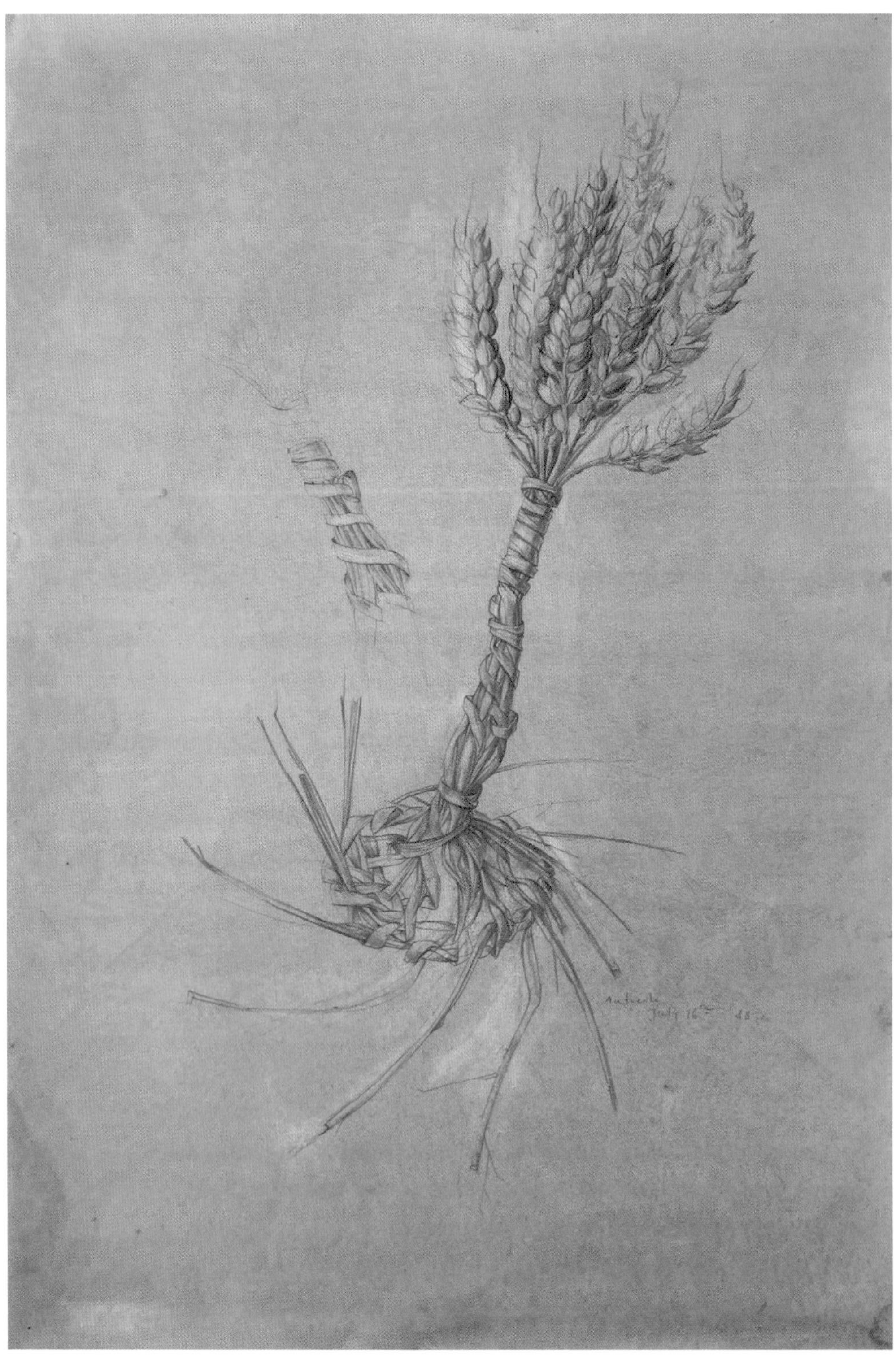

This full-size cartoon was Anne Newland's principal work during her Scholarship at The British School at Rome, which she was awarded in 1938. In correspondence with the Secretary of the School she described it as the central panel of a triptych for which she never intended to produce the side panels. The composition shows the influence of Andrea Mantegna whose works she was especially drawn to.

Ceres, according to ancient Roman myth, was the goddess of agriculture, grain crops, fertility and motherly relationships. Newland returned to the same composition ten years later in a related pencil drawing entitled *Composition, The Legend of Ceres*, (1949). In 1950, at The Royal Academy, Newland exhibited a variation on the theme, entitled *Three Marys*, which was loosely inspired by this earlier decorative composition.

The study of a wheatsheaf shows how Newland built up her design step by step, every element the subject of intense scrutiny. 'Anticoli' refers to the artist's community of Anticoli Corrado (located about 40 kilometres northeast of Rome) where many Rome Scholars spent the summer. On the final cartoon corrections to the design have been made in white and there are additionally accidental splashes of ink.

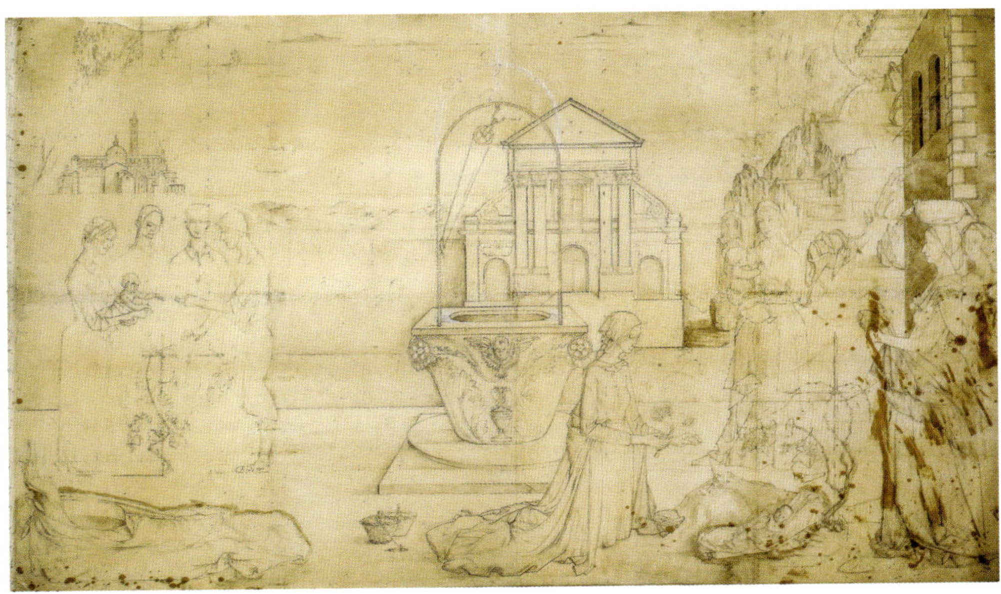

The Legend of Ceres, c.1938-39,
full-size cartoon, pencil and wash with wash, with corrections in white and splashes of ink on tracing paper,
45 ¼ x 75 in. (114.5 x 191 cm).

Study for *The Legend of Ceres, (Anticoli)*, inscribed and dated 'July 16th Anticoli 48',
pencil on grey paper, 17 ½ x 12 in. (44 x 30 cm).

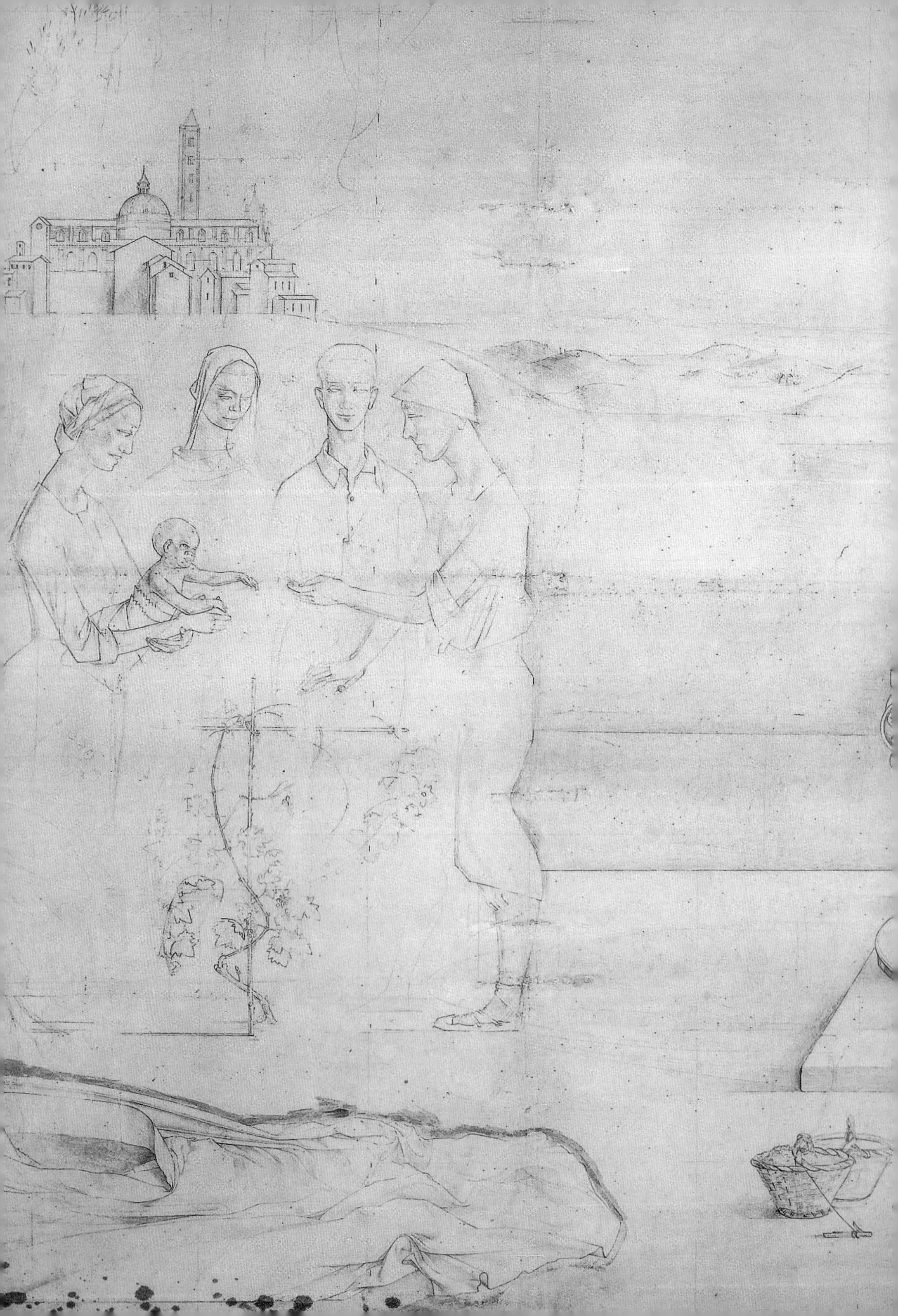

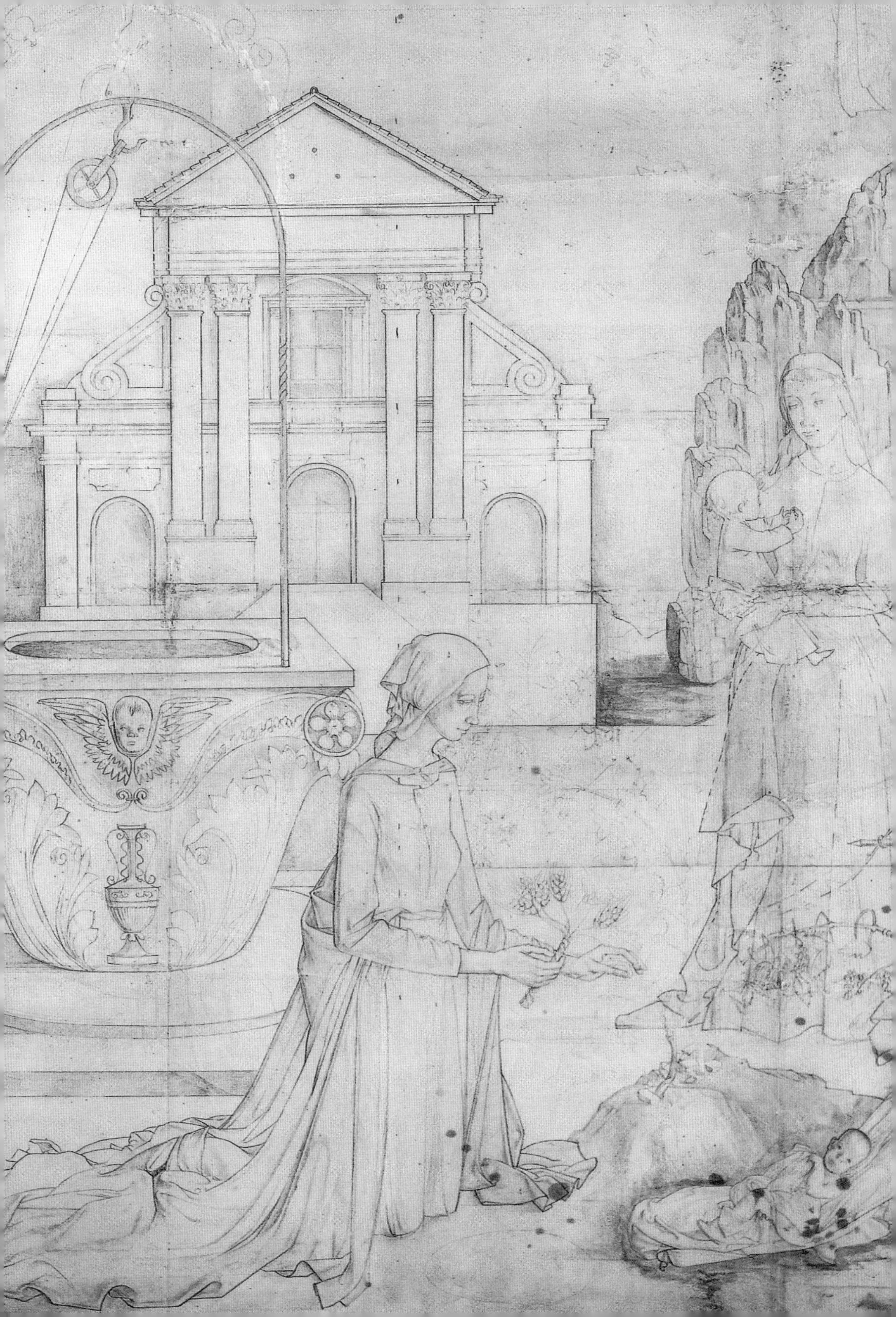

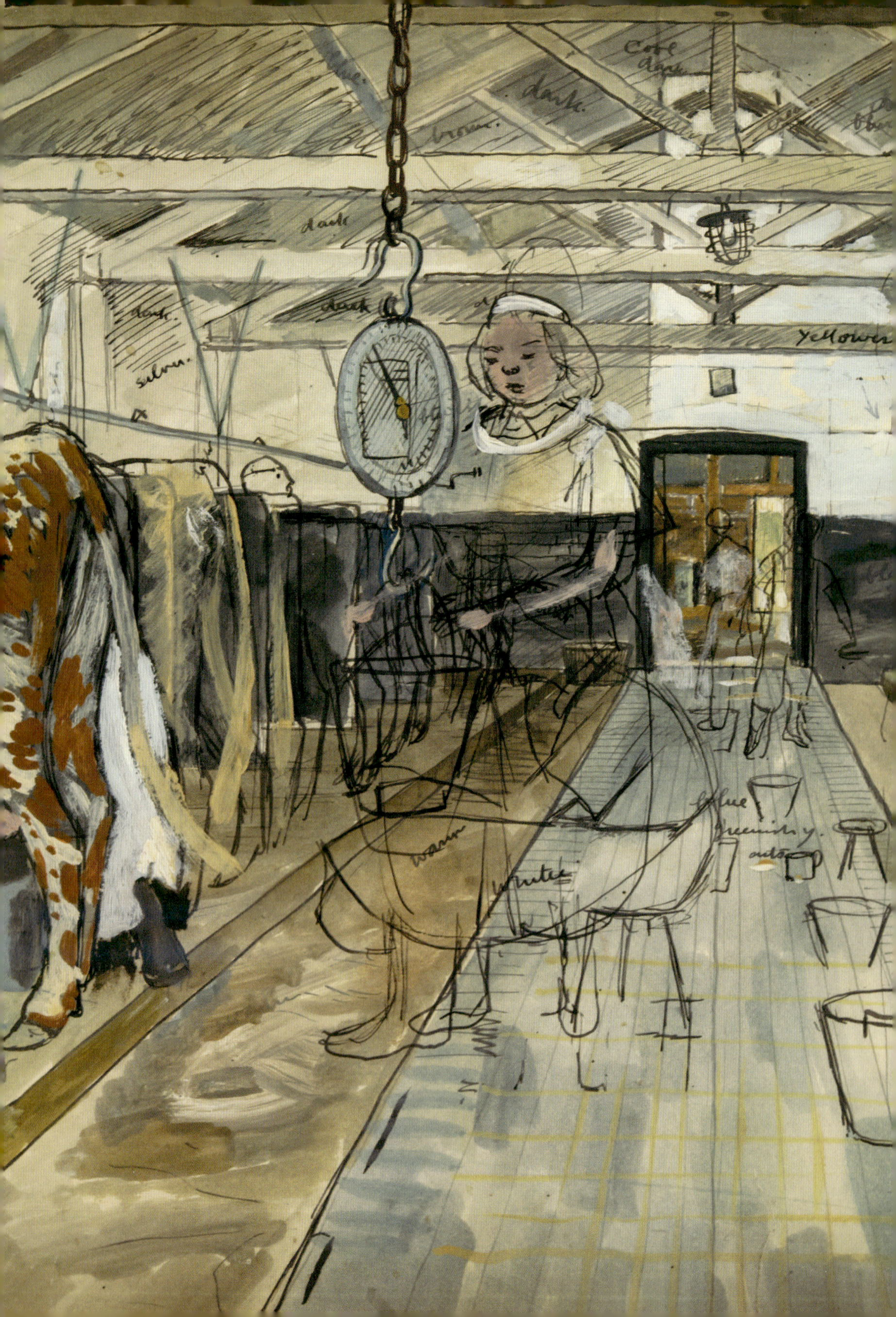

In May 1940, Evelyn Dunbar, the only woman to receive a full-time salary from the War Artists' Advisory Committee (WAAC), was posted to Sparsholt Farm Institute, near Winchester, to paint Women's Land Army recruits in training. Painted around the time Dunbar was considering how to illustrate *A Book of Farmcraft*, her painting *Milking Practice with Artificial Udders* (see overleaf) shows three novice Land Girls, struggling to learn the rudiments of milking. The Land Girl in the middle has assumed the recommended posture. The painting is squared for transfer – it is a study for the nearly identical finished painting in the Imperial War Museum.

In *Study for Women's Land Army Dairy Training*, operations have moved from artificial to real. Dunbar's perspective lines lead the viewer to the dairy wash-house beyond, itself the setting for *Milking Practice with Artificial Udders*. The extensive colour notes would have served as an aide-memoire to guide her when she returned to her studio in Rochester to work the sketch up. However, Dunbar appears to have never completed this composition and she later used the same title *Women's Land Army Dairy Training* for a different WAAC commission. By September 1943, a quarter of the 80,000-strong Women's Land Army were involved in milking.

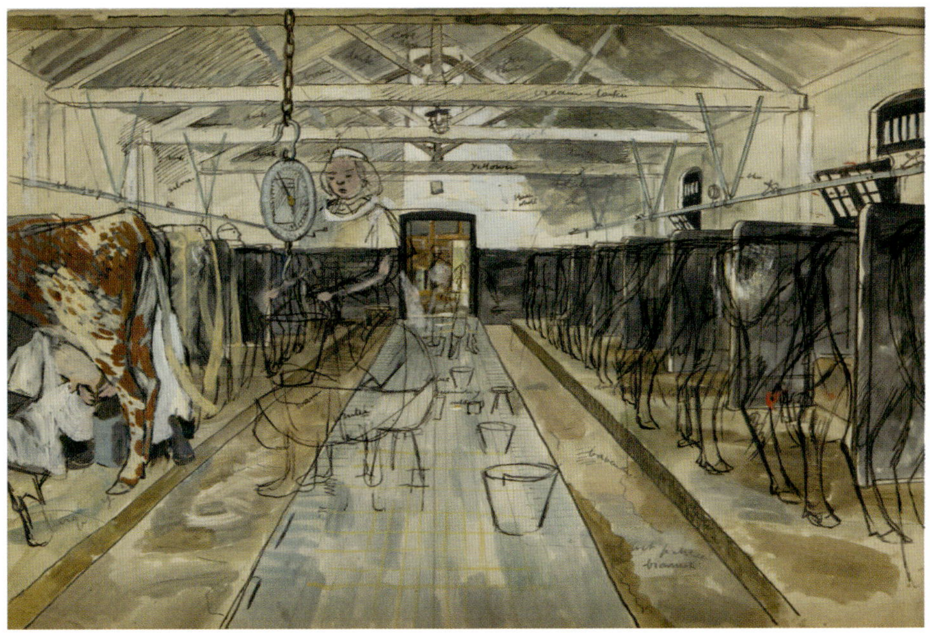

Study for *Women's Land Army Dairy Training*, 1940, inscribed with title and notes, thinned oil over pen & ink on paper, 14 ¼ × 21 in. (36 × 53.5 cm).

OVERLEAF:
Milking Practice with Artificial Udders, 1940,
oil on paper, squared, laid on board, 22 × 30 in. (55.8 × 76.2 cm).

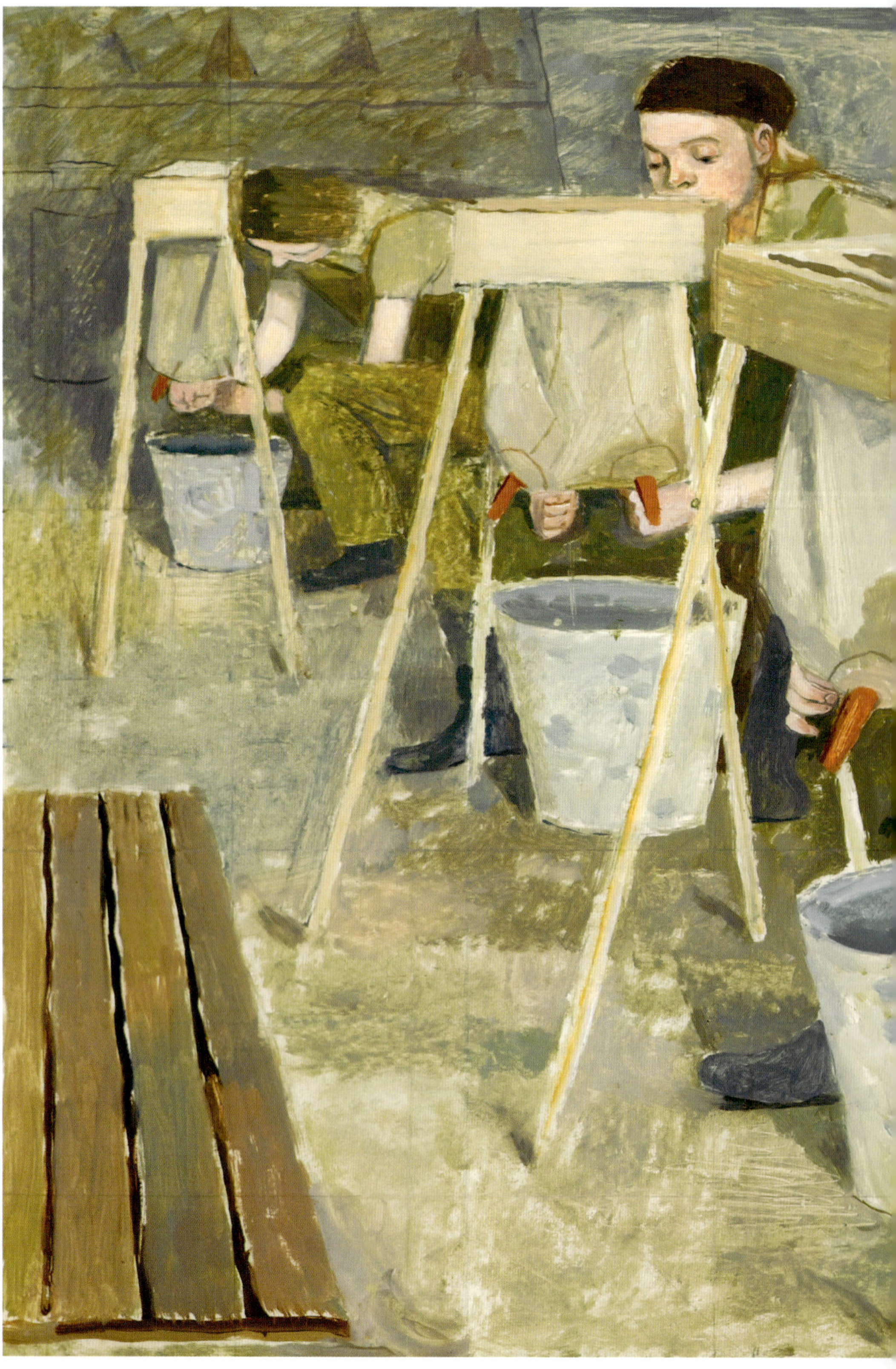

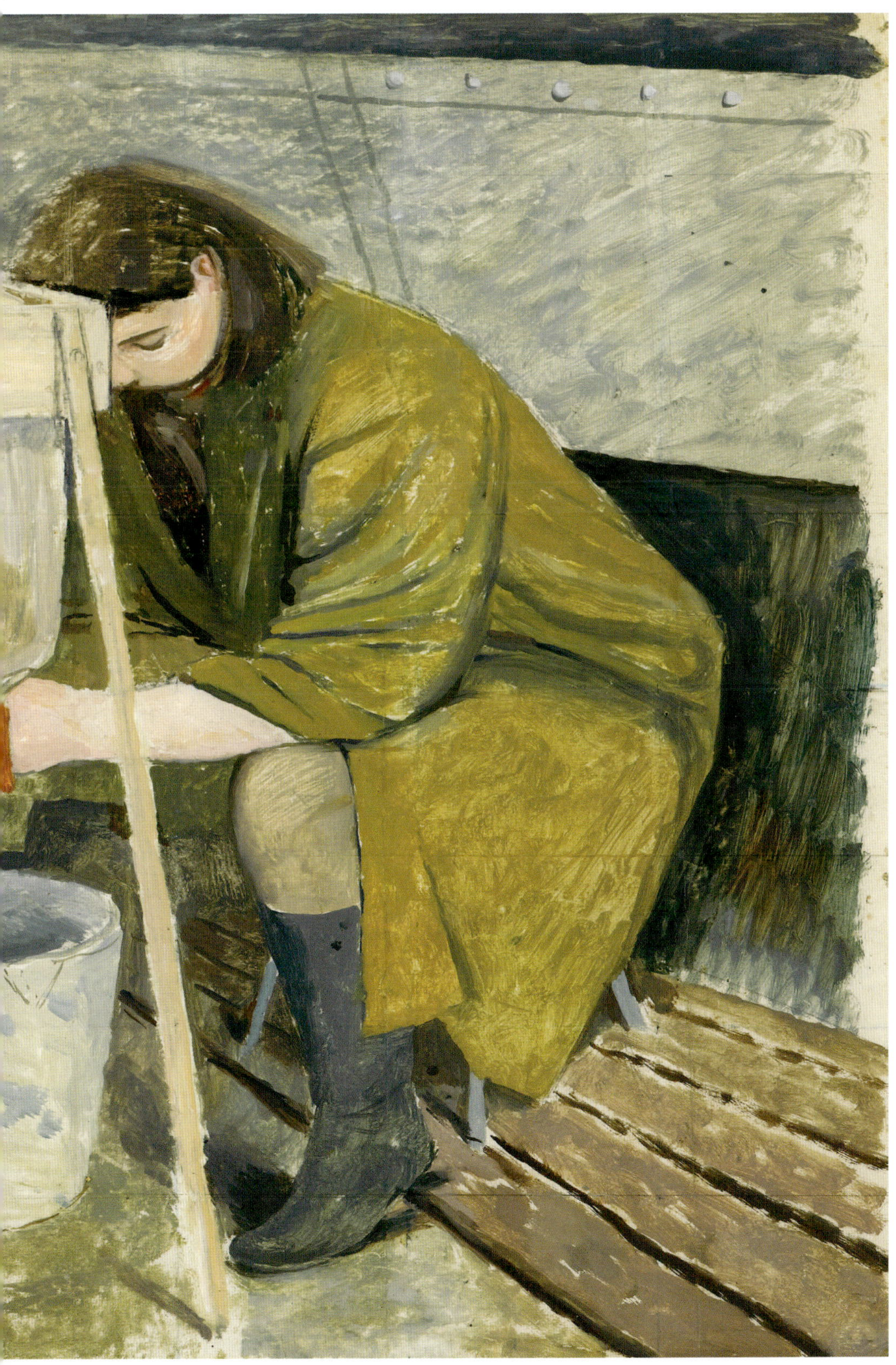

Clare Leighton (1898-1989)

The original woodblocks *Hog Killing and Apple Butter* were produced for Clare Leighton's iconic book *Southern Harvest* (published in New York, 1942, by The Macmillan Company). *Southern Harvest* comprised over 35 vignettes depicting, amongst other subjects picking cotton, shucking corn, boiling sorghum and harvesting tobacco – all part of the rich agricultural heritage of America's South. It was amongst her most important achievements, providing a unique and poignant record of rural life of the period. Leighton would often take an entire week to produce a wood engraving, the formative ideas worked up in a pencil sketch, (see overleaf) which would then be drawn directly on to a naked block covered in Chinese white. The design was then painstakingly carved with tools strong enough to incise into the end grain of the block, which was typically made of boxwood, sufficiently hard to allow for a number of prints to be made before any loss of sharpness. 'Fortunately the boxwood block, unlike the copper plate, will yield an almost indefinite number of perfect prints', Clare Leighton wrote in her book *Wood-Engraving and Woodcuts* in 1932. From each block a limited edition of 50 numbered and signed wood engravings were produced. For the publication, a lithographic process was used.

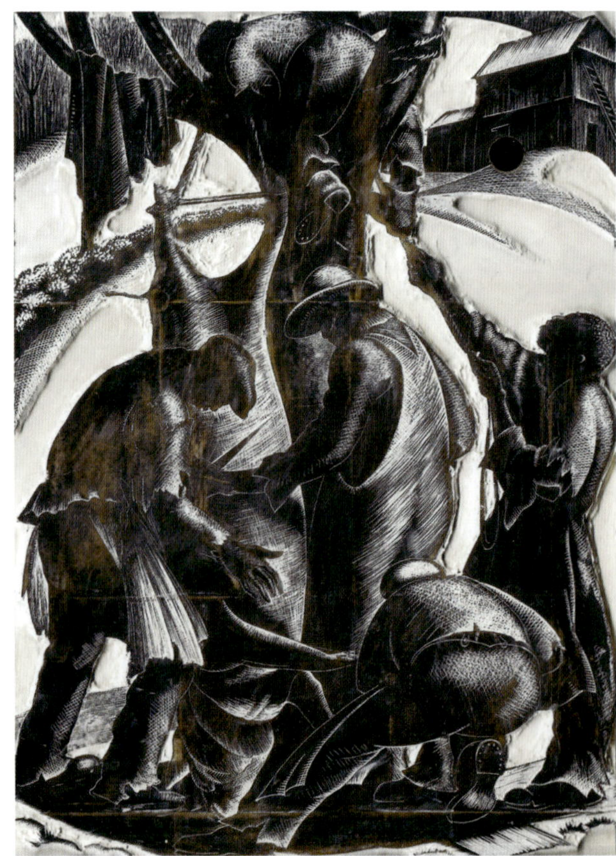

Hog Killing (BPL 514), c.1942,
from *Southern Harvest*,
original woodblock
coloured with gesso (cancelled),
7 ½ x 5 ¼ in. (19 x 13.4 cm).
Southern Harvest was published
by The Macmillan Company,
New York, 1942.

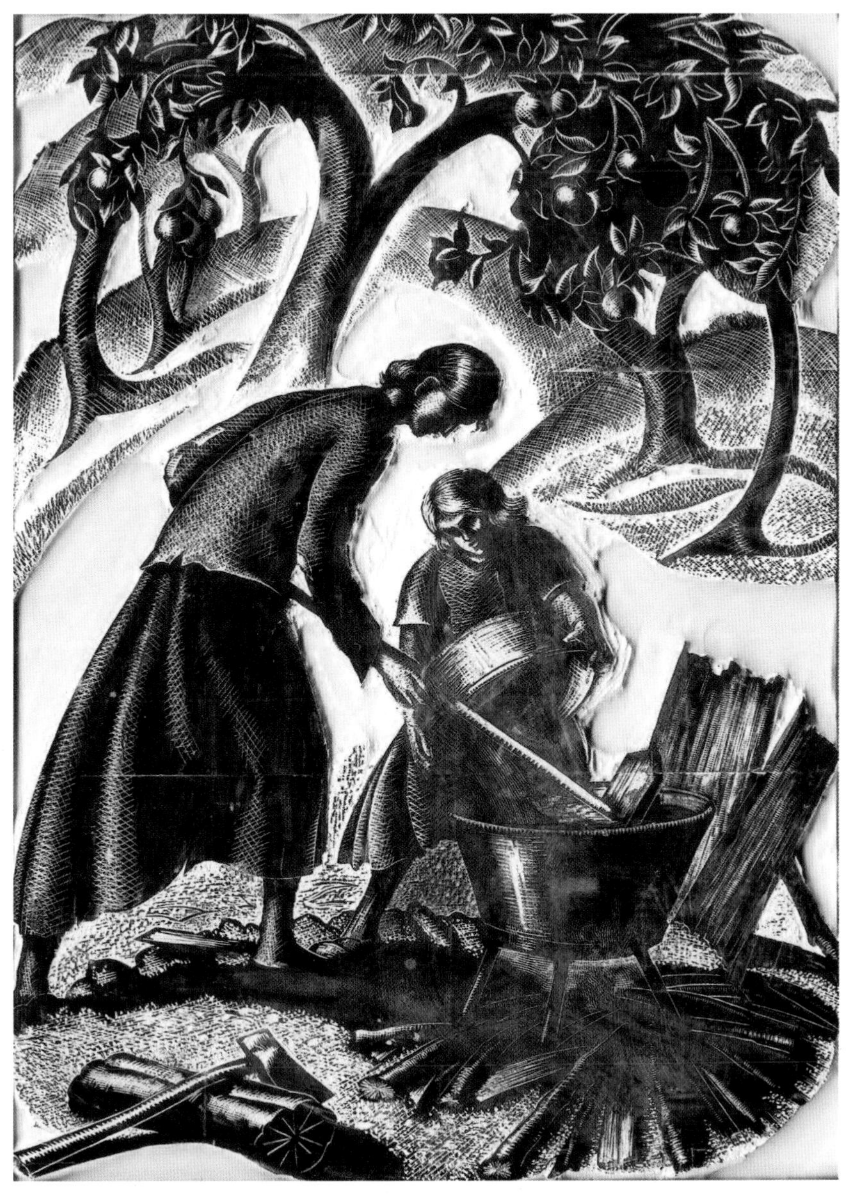

Apple Butter (BPL 523), c. 1942, from *Southern Harvest,*
original woodblock coloured with gesso (cancelled), 7 ½ × 5 ¼ in. (19 × 13.4 cm).

OVERLEAF:
Apple Butter (page from maquette for *Southern Harvest*), c.1942,
pencil on paper, full sheet: 8 ½ × 11 in. (21.4 × 28 cm).

Hill Folks

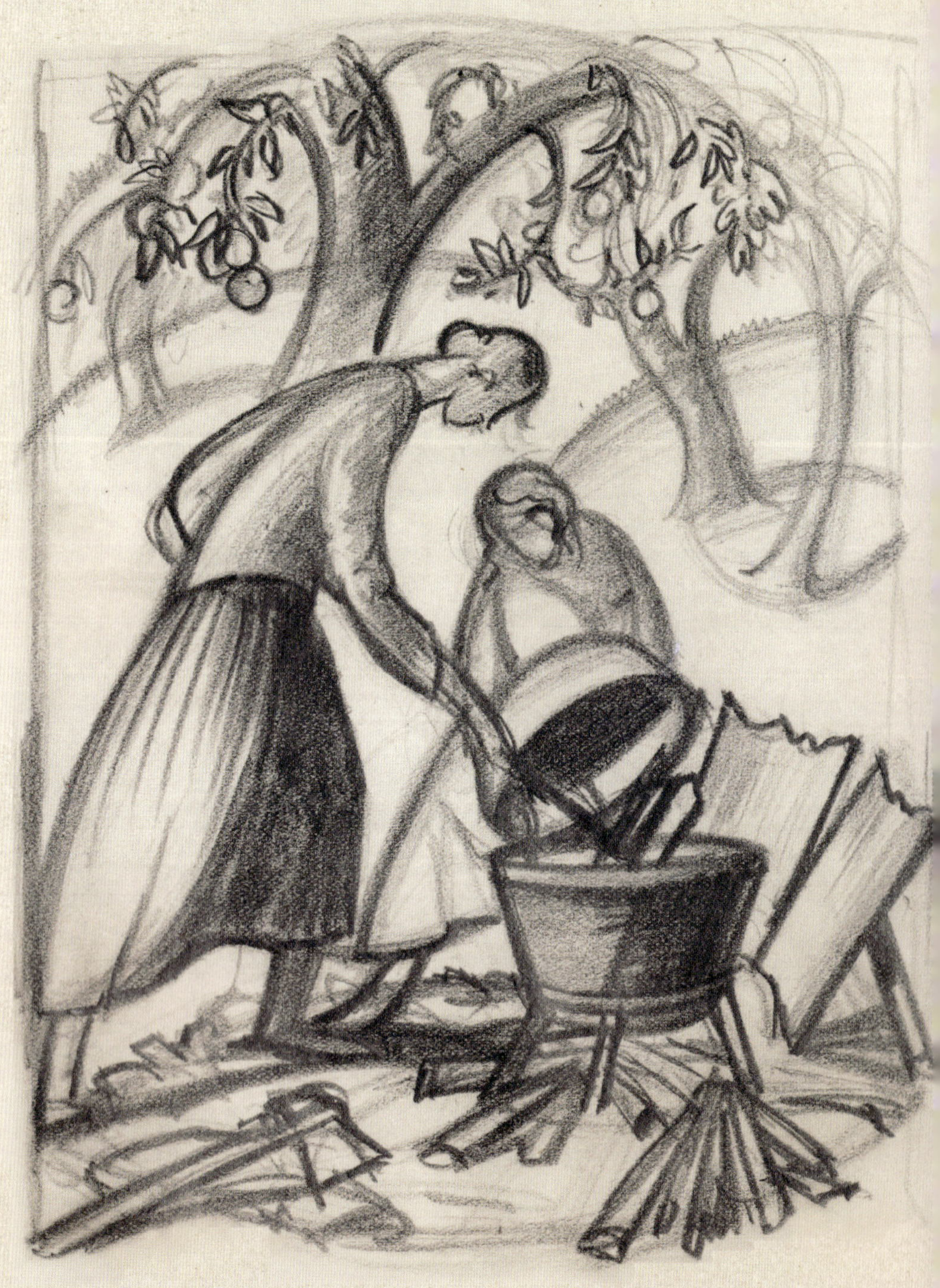

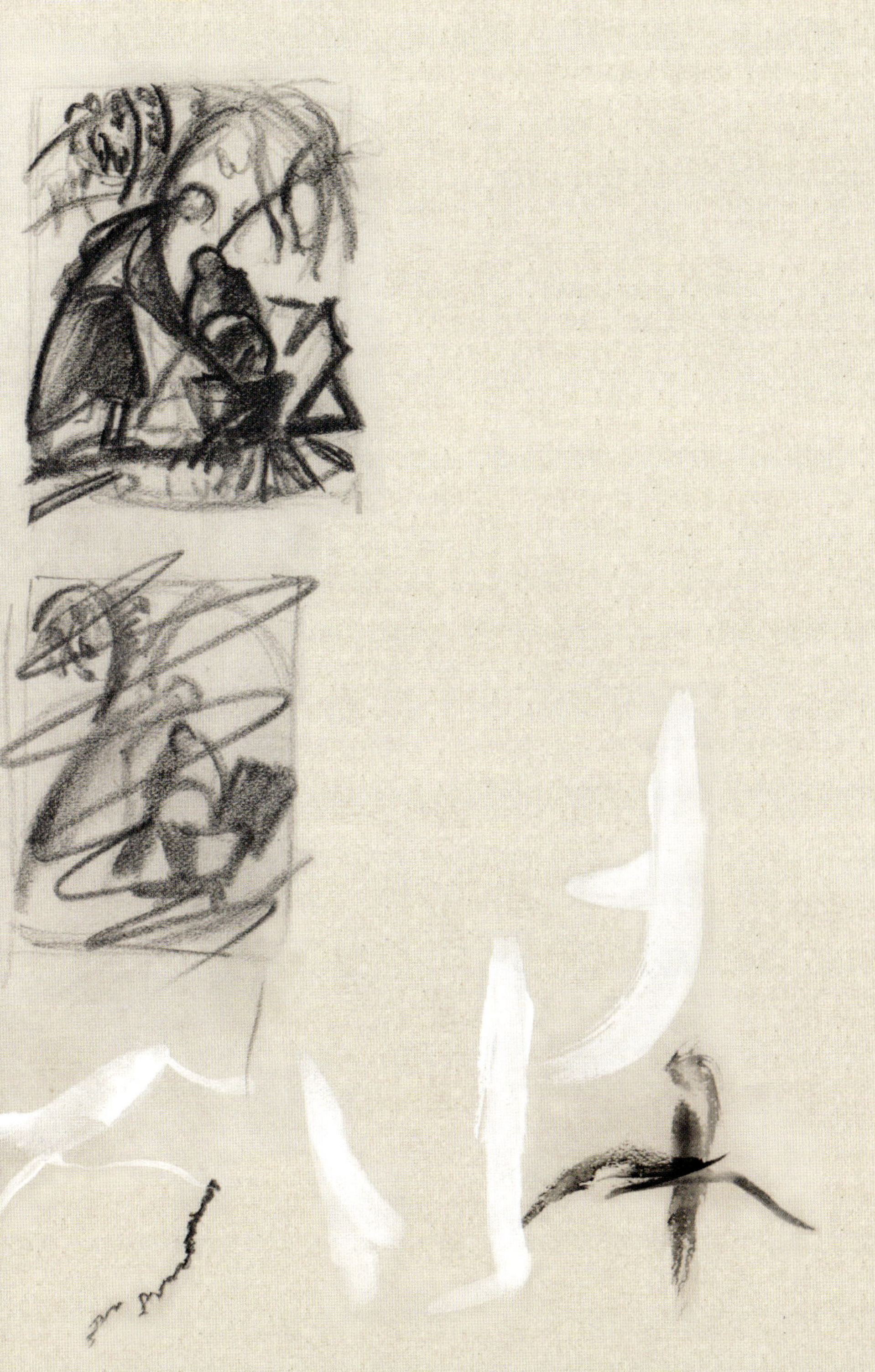

Phyllis Ginger (1907-2005)

This brutally honest self-portrait can be dated to Phyllis Ginger's student years at the Central School of Art, where, having been awarded a scholarship, she studied under William P Robins. She had recently left her civil service clerking job – a career path that her parents had persuaded her to take – and had cut her long auburn hair short. Leafing through a sketchbook, and engaging the viewer with a bold and penetrating gaze, Ginger asserts herself as an independent artist. This is a rare self-image; Eleanor Durbin, the artist's daughter, declared that 'portraying friends and family members was much more in Ginger's character. She was interested in recording others and was more generally self-effacing about her own image on paper'. With her heart set on a career in illustration, Ginger became a member of the Senefelder Club in 1939, and during the war produced work for the Recording Britain project. In the 1950s she illustrated numerous books and exhibited etchings with the Royal Society of Painter-Etchers and Engravers and at the Royal Academy.

Although Ginger made designs for Wedgwood plates, and 17 preparatory sketches are in the collection of the Imperial War Museum, no designs went into production. During the war, supplies of paper were limited, and the brown discolouration of this proof is due to the paper's high content of acidic wood pulp.

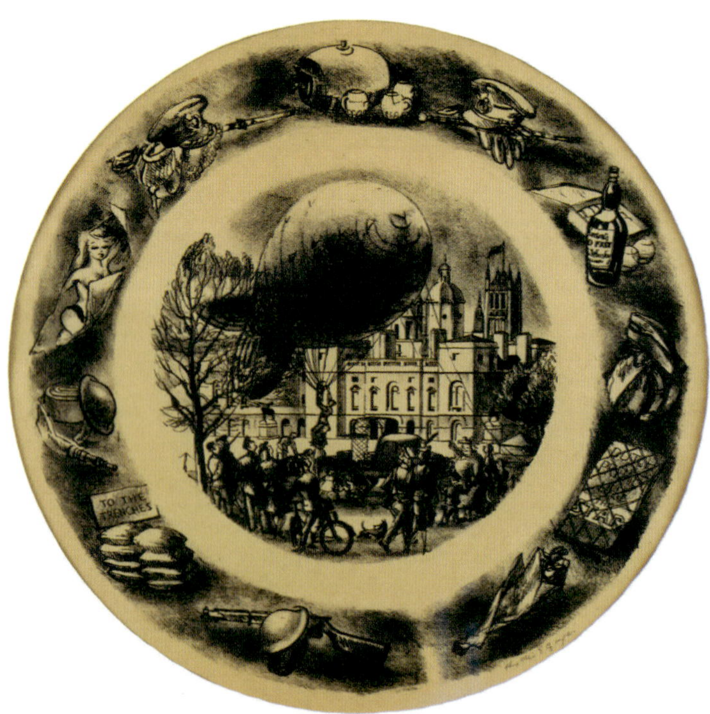

Design for a Wedgwood plate, c.1944,
trial lithographic proof on paper, 12 x 12 in. (30 x 30 cm)

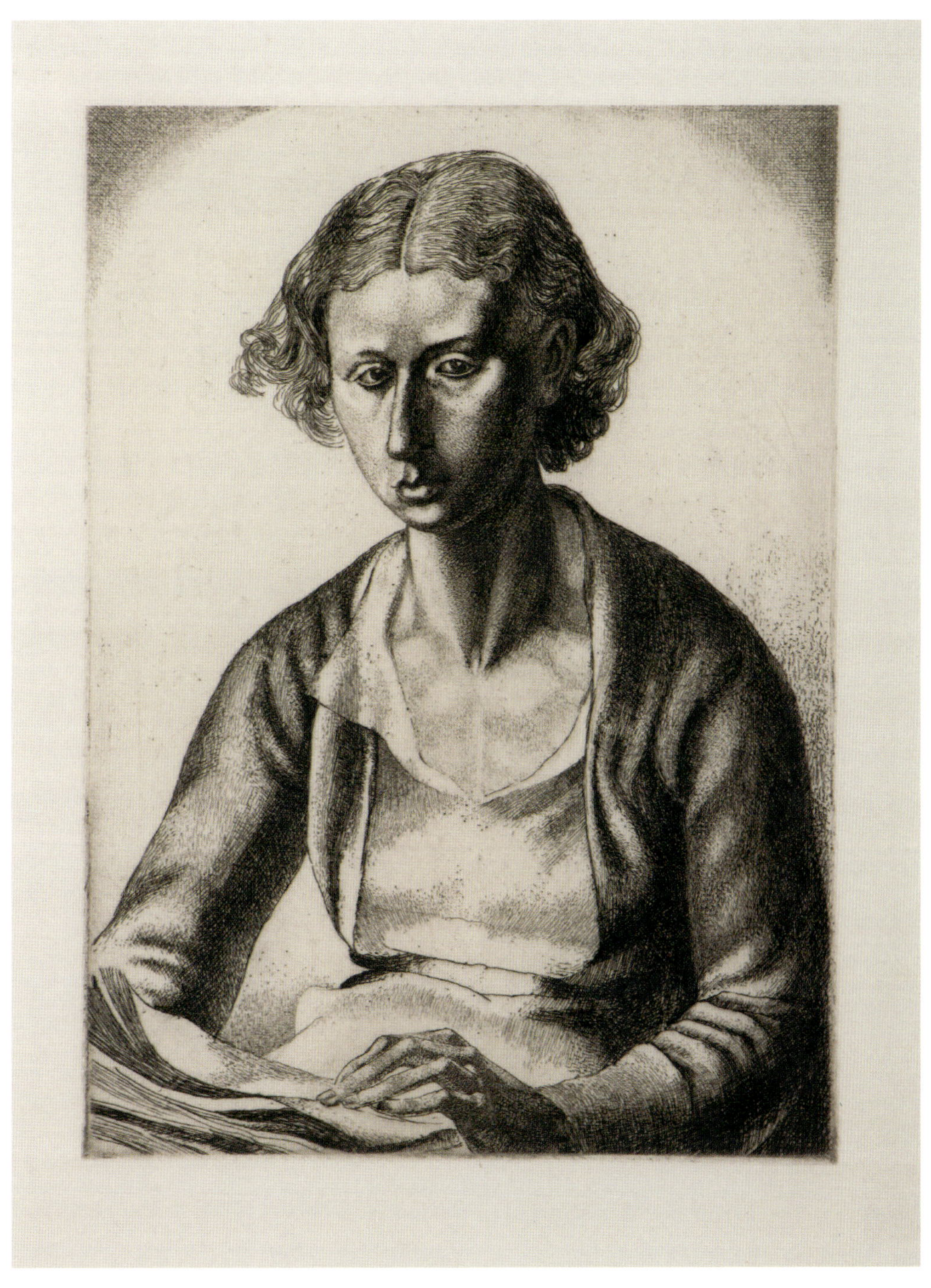

Self-portrait, c.1937,
etching on paper, plate size: 7 × 5 in. (17.8 × 12.7 cm).

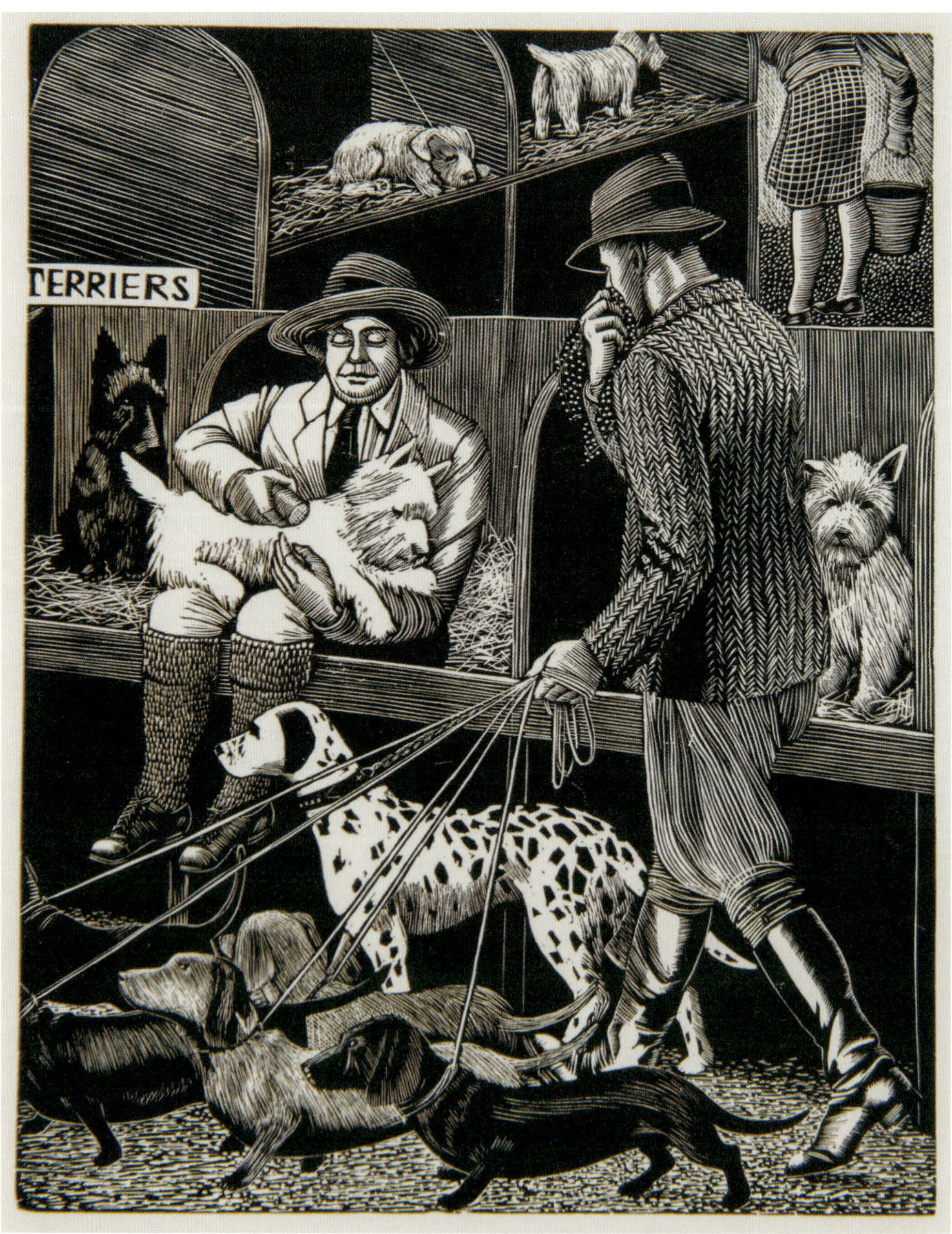

The Dog Show, 1929,
engraving printed from the original block in 1989 in an edition of 500 on 225gsm Zerkall mould-made
paper by Merivale Editions, 11 ½ × 8 ¼ in (29.3 × 20.7 cm).

Tirzah Garwood (1908-1951)

In 1925, at the age of 17, Tirzah Garwood enrolled at Eastbourne School of Art, where, under the instruction of her young tutor, Eric Ravilious, (whom she would marry five years later), she excelled in wood engraving. Her satirical scenes of bourgeois life in 1920's Britain explored themes such as bathers on Eastbourne beach, window cleaners and plump ladies shopping in Kensington. By 1927, she was already exhibiting and attracting attention for her work, and received prestigious commissions from the BBC and the Curwen Press. *The Crocodile* and *The Dog Show* were commissioned in 1929 by Oliver Simon for a projected but never completed calendar to have been published by the Curwen Press. Both engravings, however, were shown at the English Wood Engraving Society's 1929 exhibition to critical acclaim. *The Queen* (25th December 1929) compared 'the puckish humour' of Garwood's work to that of Honoré-Victorin Daumier, describing *The Dog Show* as 'wicked' and *The Crocodile* as 'that amusing bit of observation', while *Apollo* (January 1930) wrote, 'Miss Tirzah Garwood is, as one expects it of her by now, intensely amusing, especially in *The Dog Show*'.

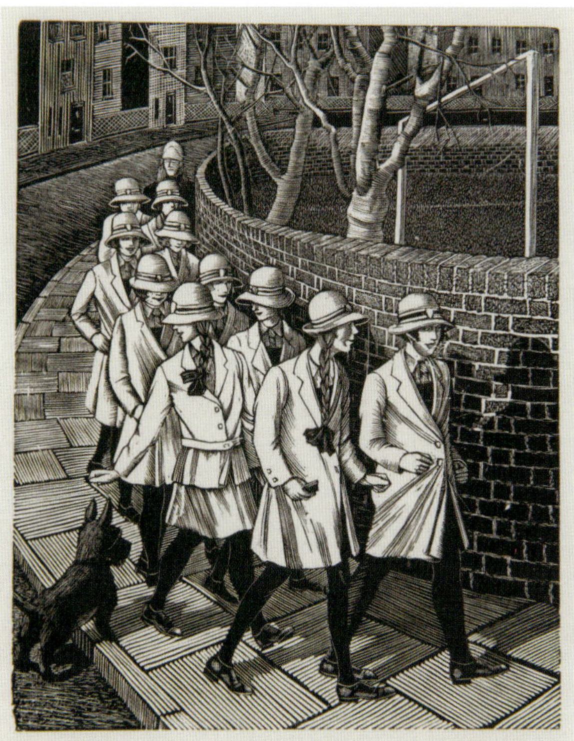

The Crocodile, 1929,
engraving printed from the original block in 1989 on 225gsm
Zerkall mould-made paper by Merivale Editions,
11 ½ x 8 ¼ in (29.3 x 20.7 cm).

Dorothy Mahoney (1902-1984)

Dorothy Mahoney (née Bishop) entered the School of Design at the Royal College of Art in 1924 with Book Illustration as her principal subject. From 1926-28 she also took classes in lettering and illumination with Edward Johnston, to whom she became student-assistant. Students were encouraged to copy early English manuscripts from the golden age of calligraphy. This page is copied from the English 14th century Queen Mary Psalter, the original of which is in the British Museum but the facsimile made in 1912 is held in the Victoria and Albert Museum next to the Royal College of Art. Mahoney's book, *The Craft of Calligraphy* (1982) was, and remains, one of the standard reference works on the subject.

In *Walled Garden Amongst Kentish Orchards*, Mahoney's skill in illumination and penmanship is shown in the precise delineation of the tulip petals and trellis work.

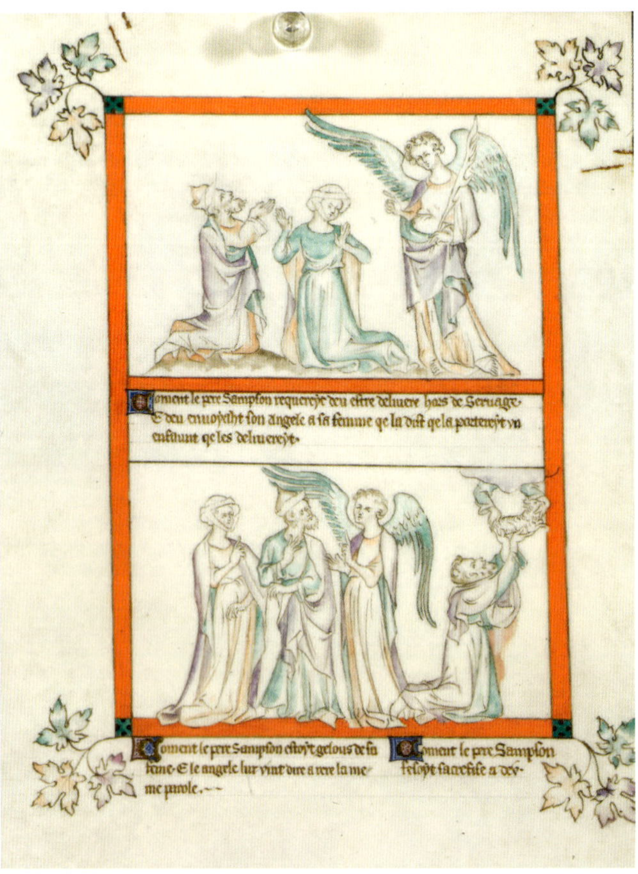

Study from the *Queen Mary Psalter*, late 1920s,
watercolour, ink and gold leaf on vellum, 10 ½ x 7 ½ in. (27 x 19 cm).

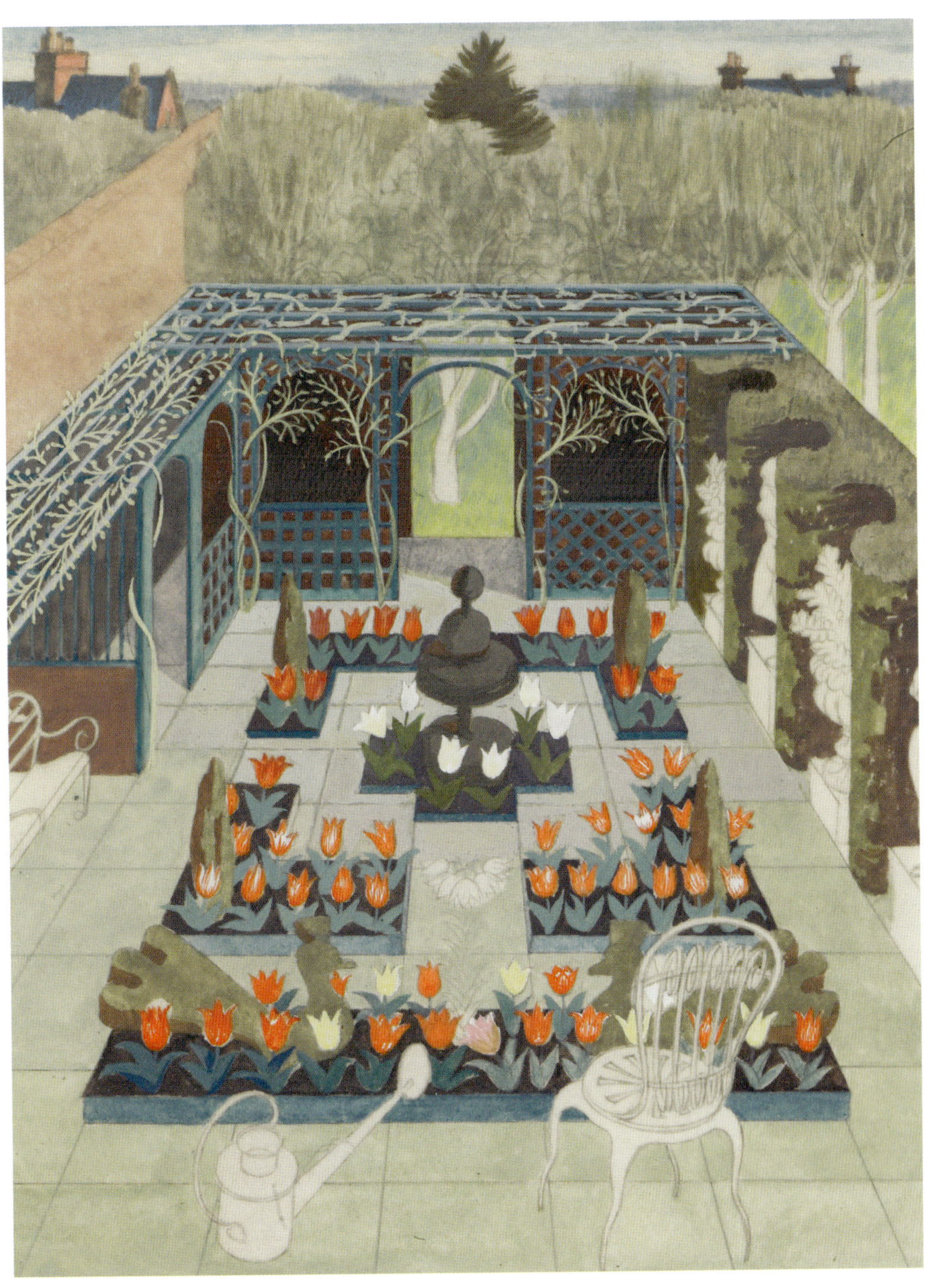

Walled Garden Amongst Kentish Orchards, early 1950s,
mixed media on vellum, 7 ½ × 5 ½ in. (19 × 14 cm).

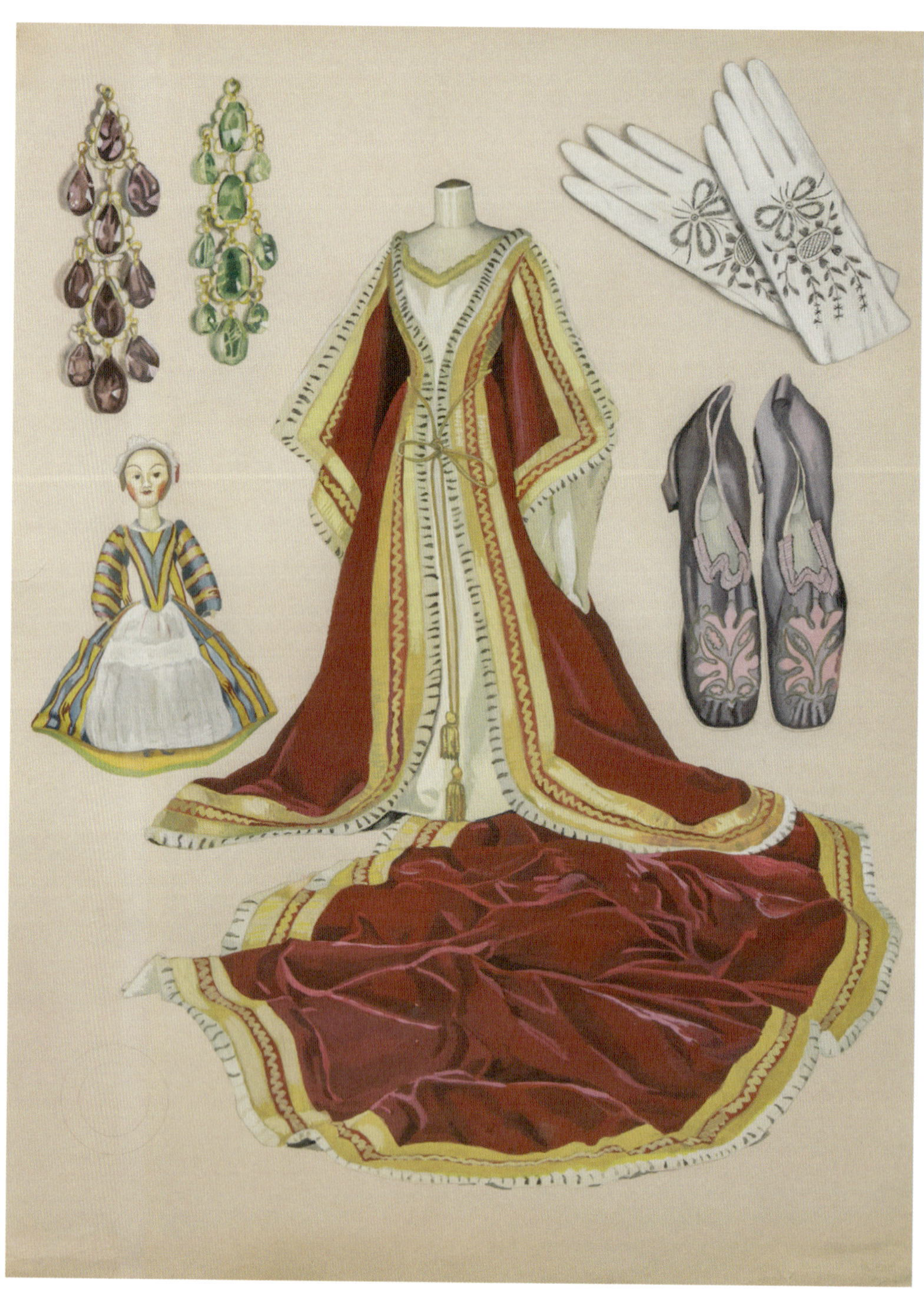

The Museum II, 1953,
watercolour, gouache and pen & ink on paper, 30 x 22 in. (76 x 56 cm)

Museum I and *Museum II* are exceptional works in Edith Rimmington's artistic production, in the sense that she never made works exceeding a 50 x 70 cm format. The pair were made following an exhibition of regalia that Rimmington saw in London in 1953, the year of the Queen's Coronation, which gave her the idea of a counter-celebration of monarchy, with subtle ironic undertones.

The King is represented with a gauntlet – the symbol of power and a challenge of combat (to throw down the gauntlet). Yet the king is also shown as a chess piece (alongside the bishop and knight), and reduced to a part in a game beyond his control. Lastly, the anachronistic airship - one of the 'flying machines of those madmen' from the early days of aviation – may symbolise man's eternal (but doomed) desire to fly high.

The Queen is represented with lavish but useless trappings. The gloves and slippers are of no use to her; nor the tear- drop earrings, for she has no head, arms or feet. Like the king and the chess piece, the doll shows her as but a toy for some greater power.

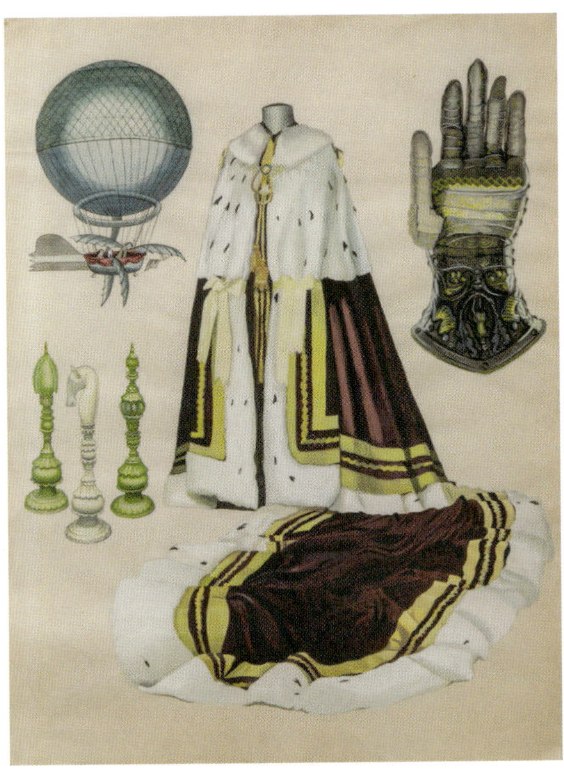

The Museum I, 1953,
watercolour, gouache and pen & ink on paper, 30 x 22 in. (76 x 56 cm).

Marion Adnams (1898-1995)

An early work, probably undertaken when Marion Adnams was at Derby School of Art, there is no record that this nautical mural, which was clearly a site-specific decoration (space is left for a doorway on the second sheet), was probably never realised. Maritime subjects inspired Adnams throughout her career; titles from her studio book typically refer to Fishing Gear, Sark, Drying the Nets etc.

From her earliest work, Adnams played with discrepancies of scale and the creation of unlikely narratives in a surrealist way. She recorded that 'When I first went to see René Magritte at the Tate I saw him for the first time and I nearly passed out. So often the same thought had been with me''.

In 1930, Adnams started attending life classes at Derby School of Art. She was gratified to find her natural ability to draw recognised, though perhaps less so in the terms her talent was acknowledged, with one teacher remarking, 'she drew like a man, direct, with no rubbing out'. The ornamental dogs featured in the pencil drawing *Study of two Staffordshire Dogs* were from Adnams' own collection of Staffordshire pottery. The addition of a piece of paper to the left-hand side, suggests that having at first intended to draw only one of the pair, Adnams felt a compulsion to unite it with its companion.

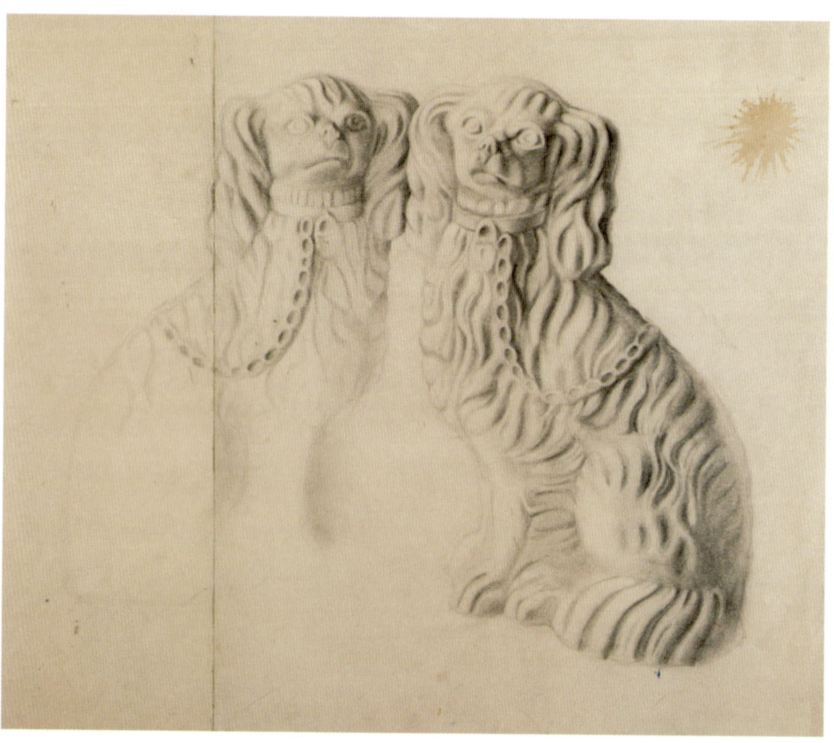

Study of two Staffordshire Dogs, c.1930,
pencil across two sheets of paper, 15 x 16 ¼ (38 x 41 cm).

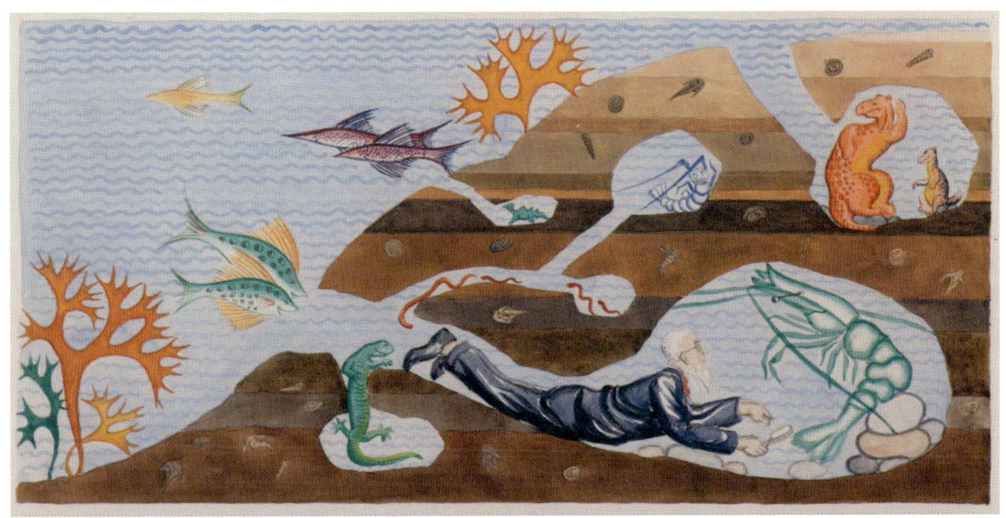

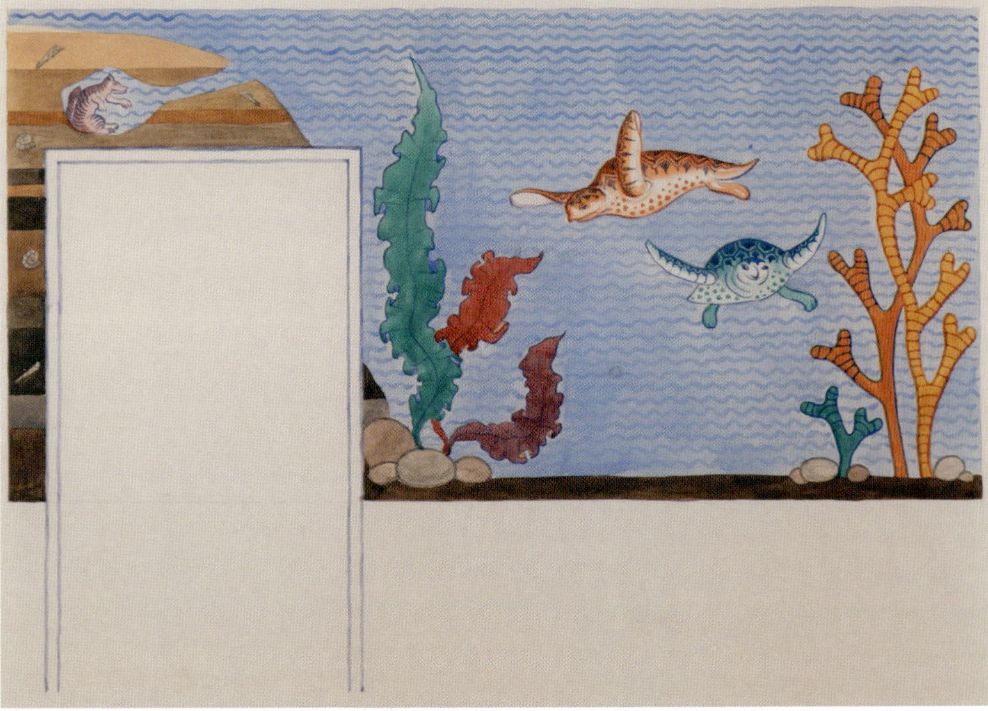

A two part design for a Nautical Mural, 1930s,
gouache on paper, each image: 5 ¾ × 11 ¾ in. (14.5 × 30 cm), each sheet: 11 ¾ × 15 ½ in. (30 × 39.5).

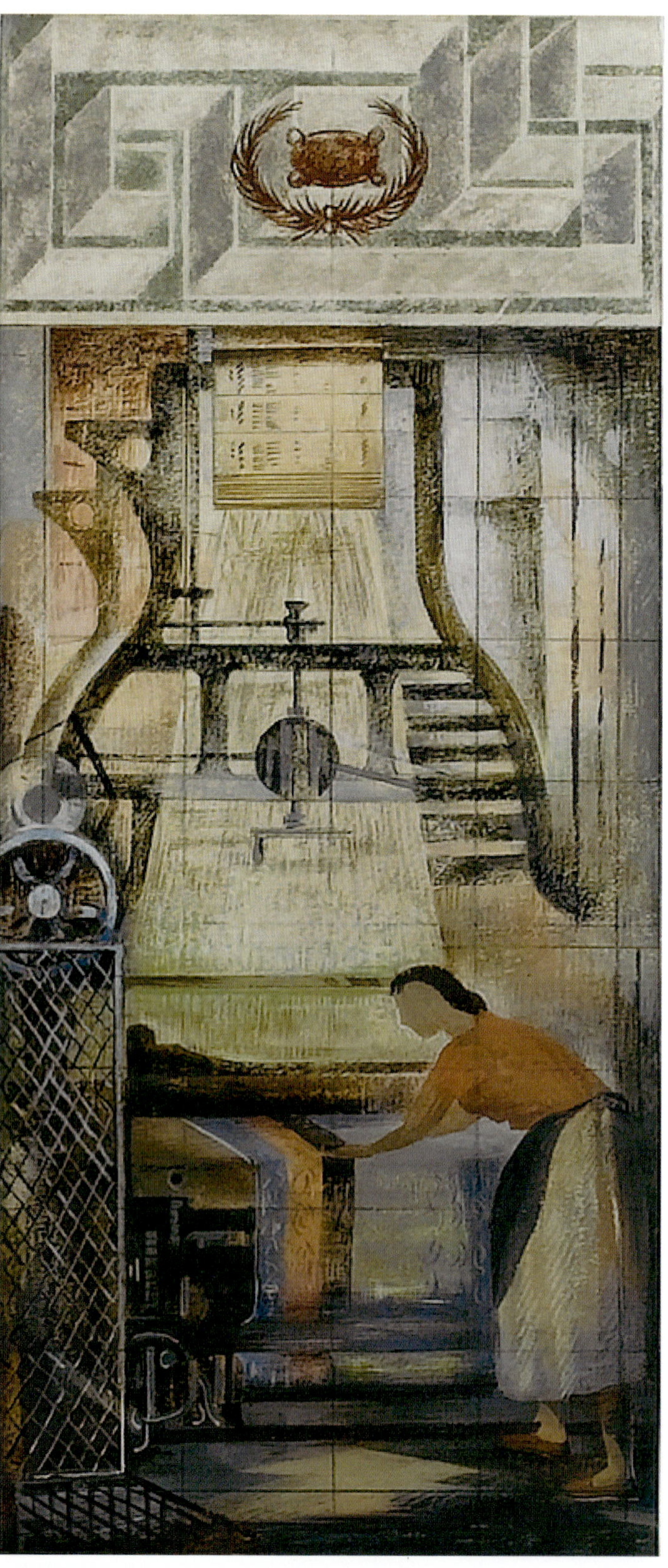

Exhibited at The Royal Academy of Arts in 1958 (933), this design in tempera was commissioned by Austen Hall, an architect and friend of the artist, for the Bankers' Clearing House, which occupied the eastern part of Coutts and Co., 15 Lombard Street, (completed in 1955 by the architectural practice of Whinney, Smith & Austen Hall). The finished mural, which measured over 6 ft in height, was worked on in Jean Clark's St. Peters Square studio. The panels depict *Transport*, *Commerce*, *Industry*, *Agriculture* and *Science*, and are flanked either side and along the top by motifs taken from token coins (used as an alternative to small change, for example by pubs or fairgrounds). When the Clearing House relocated in 1992 the original panels were removed and acquired by the Museum of London.

The term tempera refers to any painting medium consisting of coloured pigments mixed with a water-soluble binder, usually egg yolk. Typically painted on a ground prepared with gesso, tempera is characterised by the fact that it does not afford areas of impasto (textured paint) and dries quickly and therefore colours cannot be blended.

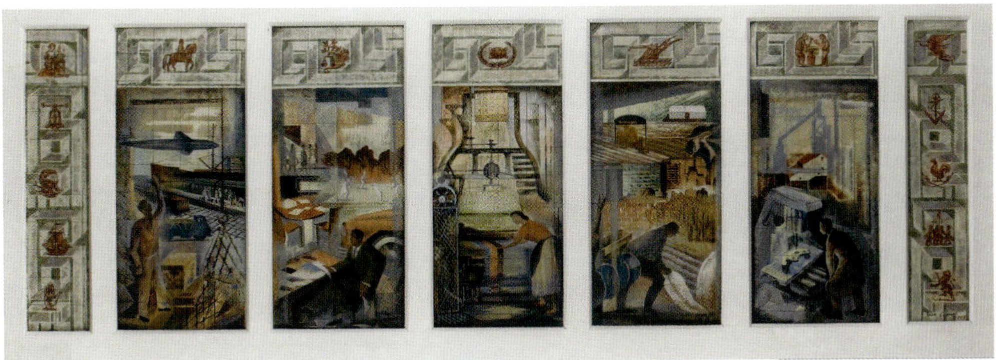

Study for a mural for the Committee Room of the London Bankers Clearing House, 1958,
signed and dated, titled on a label to the reverse,
tempera, on paper panels, squared,
two end panels: 16 ½ x 3 ½ in. (42 x 9 cm) and five central panels: 16 ½ x 7 in. (42 x 18 cm).

Kathleen Guthrie (1905-1981)

It is likely that this collage, *White, Red and Blue Circles in Square*, dates to the late 1930s when Kathleen Guthrie met John Cecil Stephenson (1889-1965), whom she married in 1941. The influence of the Circle group – whose activities centred on the Mall Studios where the couple lived – can be seen in Guthrie's design. Although Ben Nicholson and Barbara Hepworth moved to Cornwall in 1939, Henry Moore replaced them as Guthrie's immediate neighbour (taking over the lease at no. 7 Mall Studios) and Piet Mondrian became a regular visitor, living during most of the year in nearby Parkhill Road. Alexander Calder was also a frequent guest and one of his mobiles, acquired by the pair, remained hanging in their space.

Guthrie was one of the most gifted silk screen printmakers of her generation. In what might be termed a collaboration, either shortly before or after the death of Stephenson, she reproduced, as silk screens, three of his iconic *Abstracts* from 1936, 1937 and 1938.

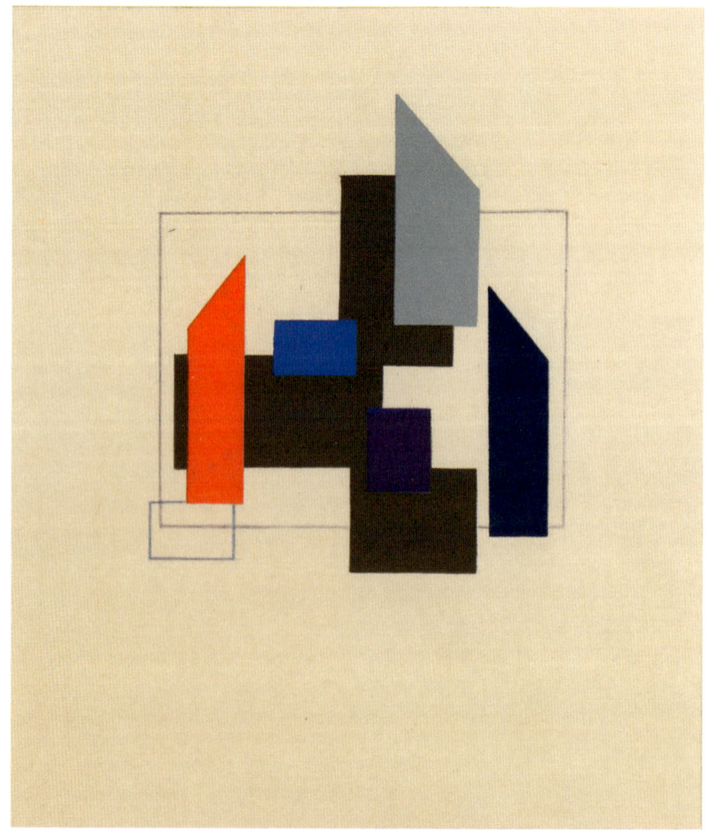

From a painting by Cecil Stephenson *1938*, c1960, signed and titled, silkscreen and crayon on paper, 11 ¾ x 9 ¾ in. (30 x 25 cm).

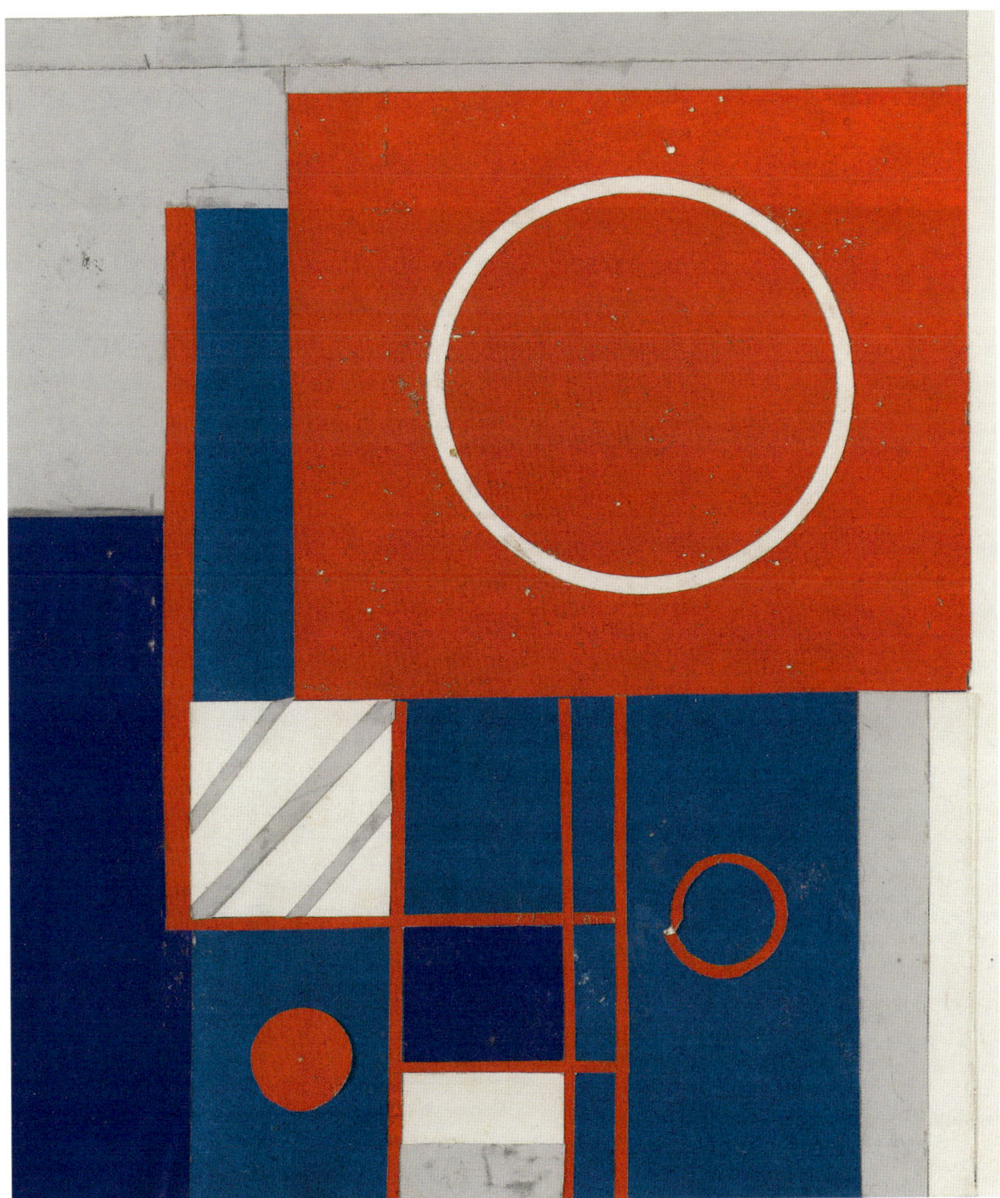

Original Design for *White, Red and Blue Circles in Square*, c. 1939,
collage and paint on paper, 9 ½ × 13 in. (24 × 33 cm).

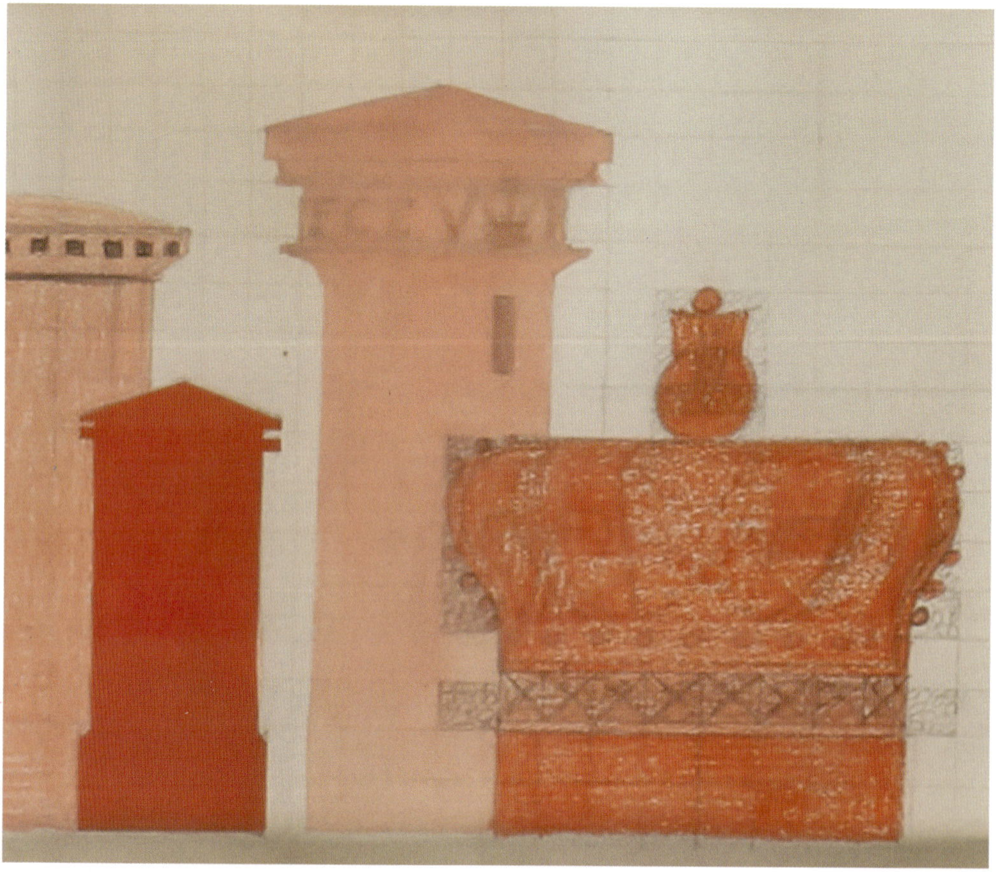

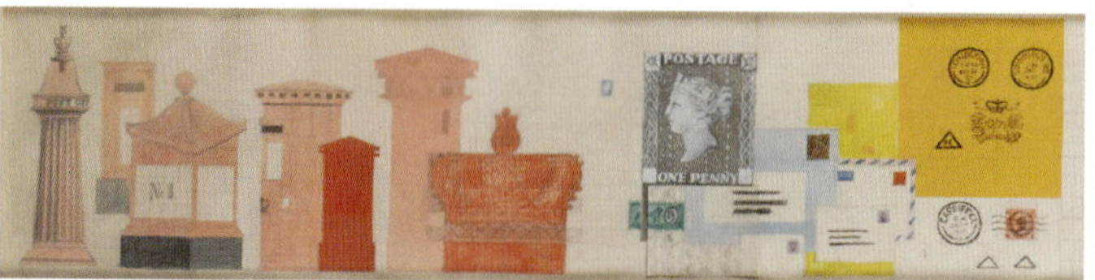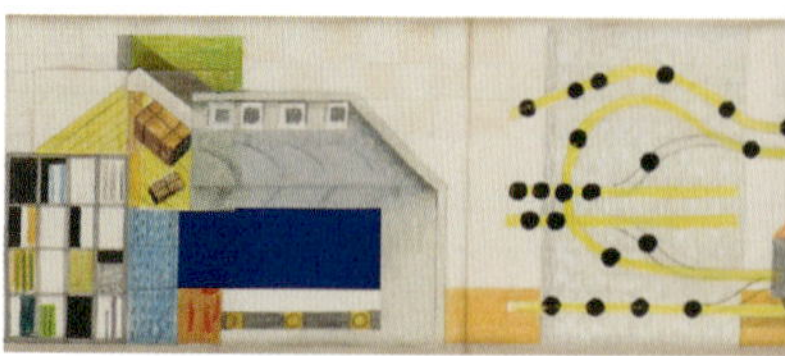

Mural design for the Royal Post Office, c.1961,
collage and crayon on paper, 9 ¾ × 120 in. (25 × 300 cm).

Barbara Jones (1912-1978)

Barbara Jones particularly loved watercolour for its translucence and brilliance and its emotive evocation of place, qualities which are evident in *Marconi Transmitting the First Radio Signals from Cornwall to Newfoundland, 1901* (overleaf), one of 12 watercolours commissioned in 1950 by the *Financial Times* for a calendar titled 'A Half Century of Progress'. By the time she received this commission, Jones' reputation was already secure, having been one of the most admired – and certainly most prolific – of the contributors to the *Recording Britain* project, a collection of more than 1500 watercolours and drawings commissioned from artists to record British lives and landscapes during the Second World War.

In her book, *Water-Colour Painting, A Practical Guide* (1960), Jones was as much concerned with engaging the reader's delight with the medium as with giving instruction in technique: 'One day when you come in … you will pour out a drink, light a cigarette, and sink into a chair, having painted a picture. Nothing in the world is like this sensation, peace and elation, God on the seventh day'.

The idea of commissioning Jones to do a mural for the Mount Pleasant sorting office in 1961 was probably inspired by the American Public Works Art Project which resulted in more than 1,200 murals being painted in post offices throughout the United States. This 3-metre long maquette is the largest record of the proposed mural – it is unclear whether this commission was ever realised.

The use of collage as a fine rather than a decorative art was one of the most significant innovations of the twentieth century, and is most associated with Picasso and Braque. The medium would have especially appealed to Jones, however, for its association with folk art. Through books such as 'The Unsophisticated Arts' (1951), she sought to blur the traditional boundaries between art, design and craft.

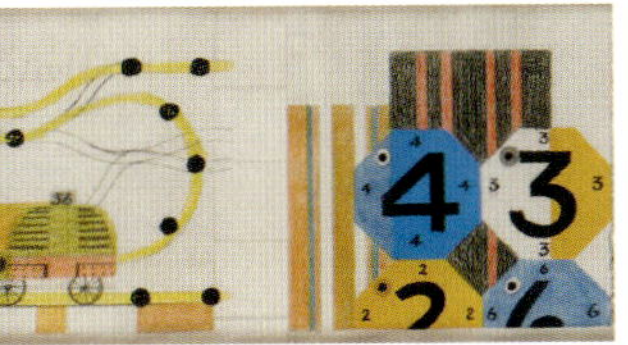

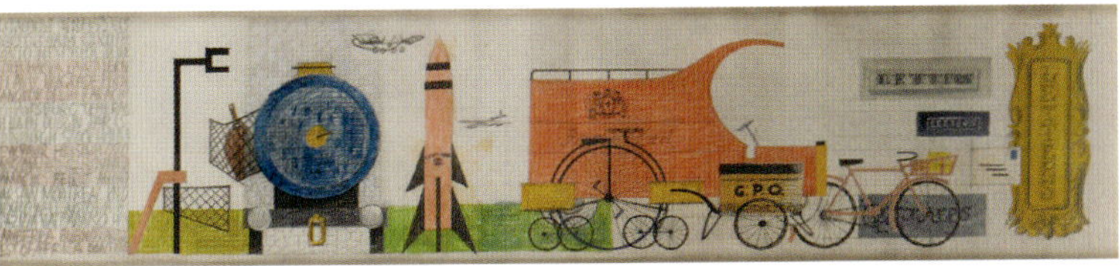

OVERLEAF:
Marconi Transmitting the First Radio Signals from Cornwall to Newfoundland, 1901, signed, watercolour and pencil on paper, 11 ¼ × 16 in. (28.5 × 40.5 cm).

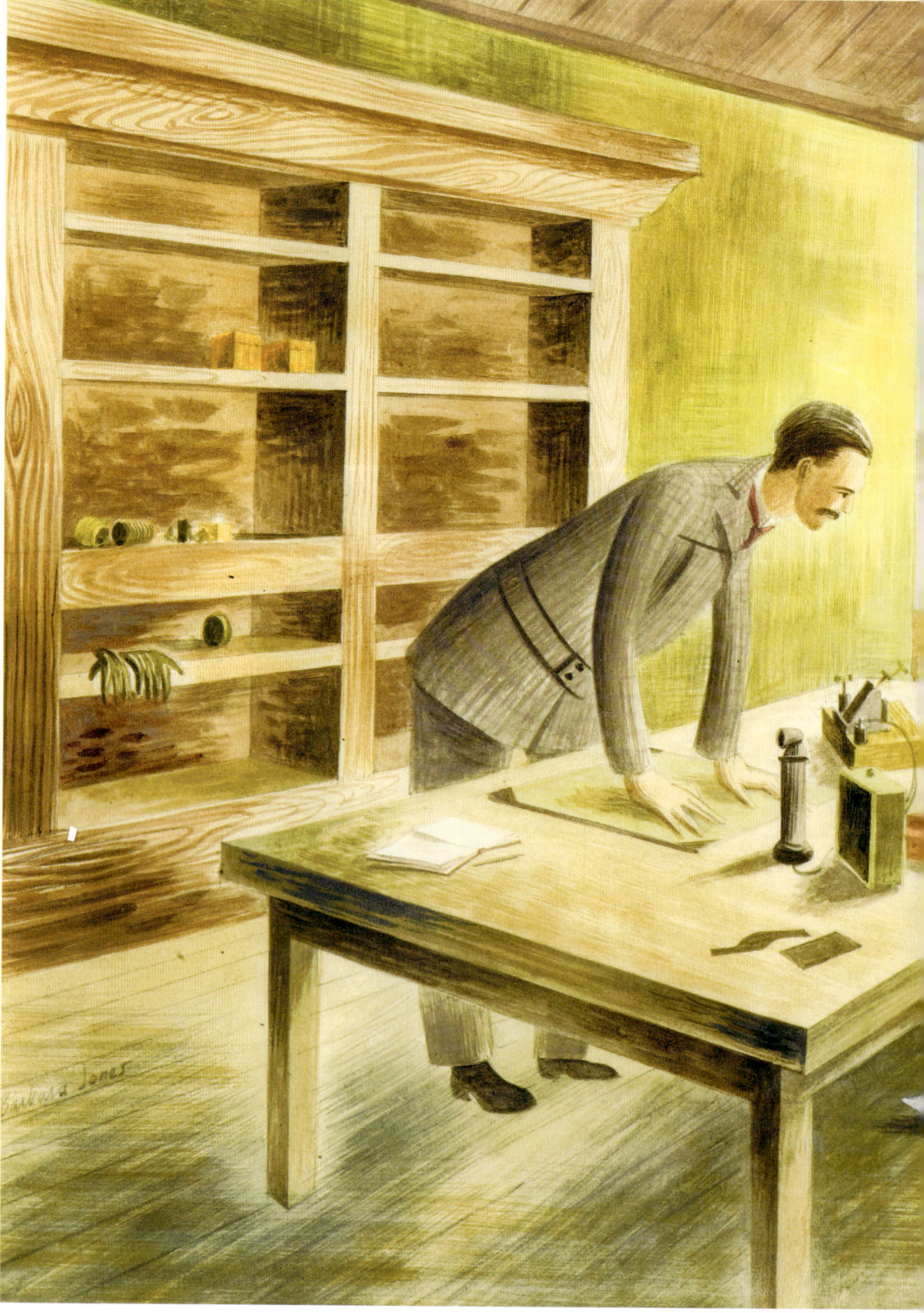

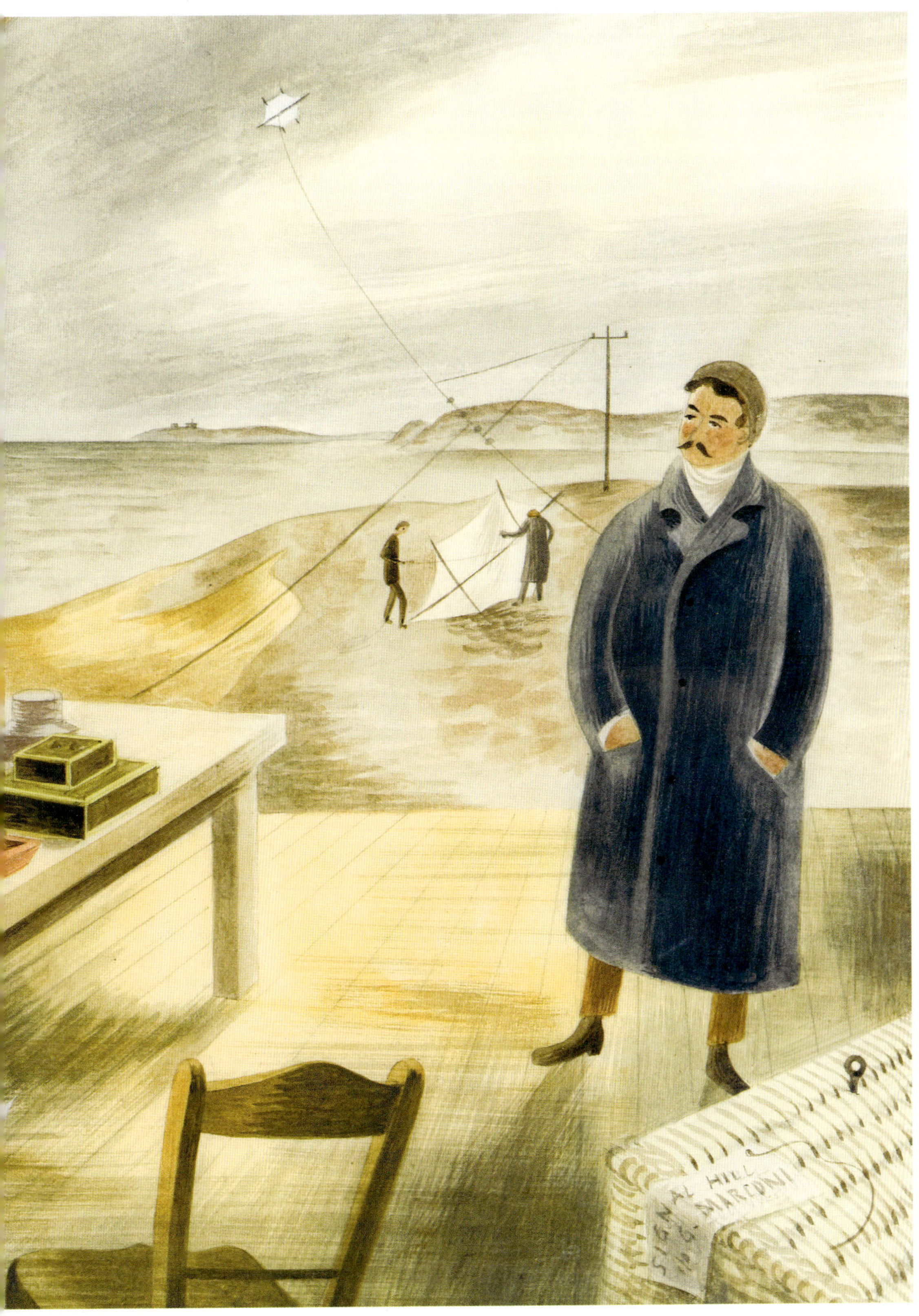
SIGNAL HILL
MARCONI

Paule Vézelay (1892-1984)

Paule Vézelay was one of the earliest and most imaginative British abstract artists. Having moved to Paris in 1926, she quickly established a visual language of non-figurative shapes and forms that she would call upon throughout the rest of her career. She insisted that the circles, ellipses, and flame-like lozenges of these works did not have their 'genesis in natural forms', but were invented according to her concerns with harmony, balance, spacing and rhythmical contrast. In 1933, Vézelay wrote: '*Of my own work I must say that I hope to give intense pleasure to the eye of the beholder, enticing his regard to remain on colours and forms more pleasing than can easily be found in actuality, or seen by his own unaided imagination. I hope this pleasure will prove a kind of music for the eyes, and may hold his regard long enough to convey what I am telling with this mysterious language of paint; since it is something that can only be painted.*'

Although adept across several mediums, Vézelay discovered what she called 'a special quality' in drawing with pastel, and often applied it directly onto canvas. Her experiments with cut-collage and pastel further demonstrate the artist's wish to express form in space from the flat surface of the paper, which she achieved in delicate and profound ways.

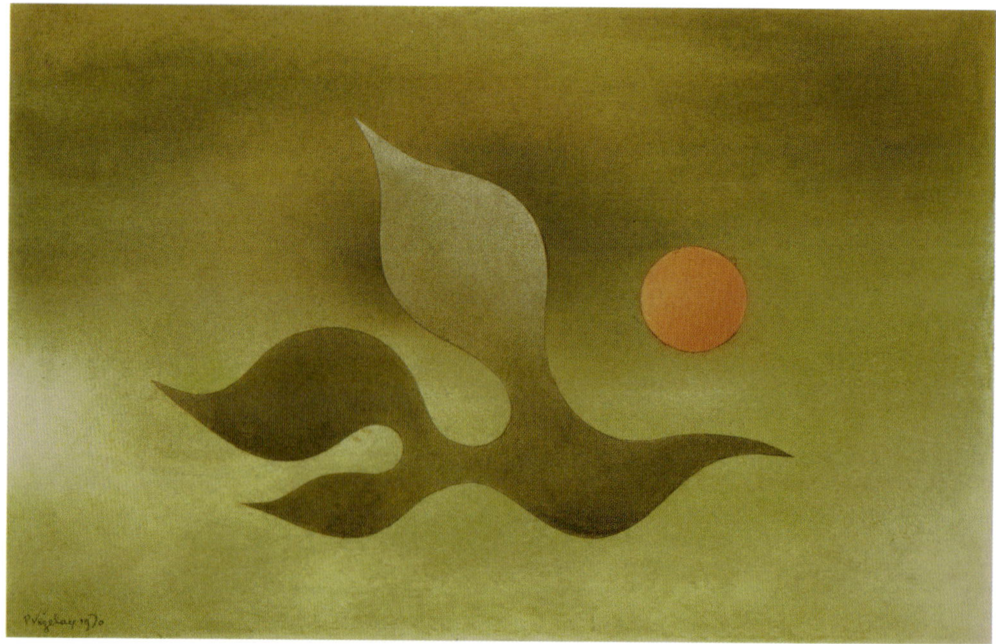

A Moving Form and a Yellow Circle, 1970, signed and dated,
collage and pastel on paper, 14 ½ x 22.¼ in. (36.8 x 56.5 cm).

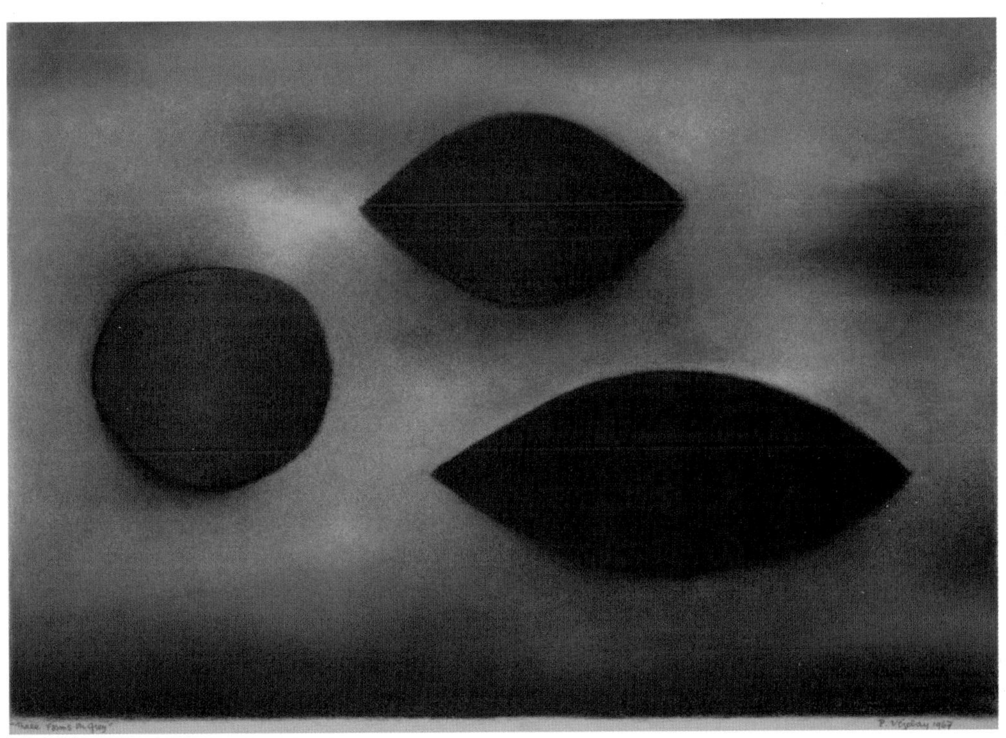

Three Forms on Grey, 1967, igned, titled and dated,
pastel on paper, 17 ¼ × 24 in. (43.8 × 61 cm).

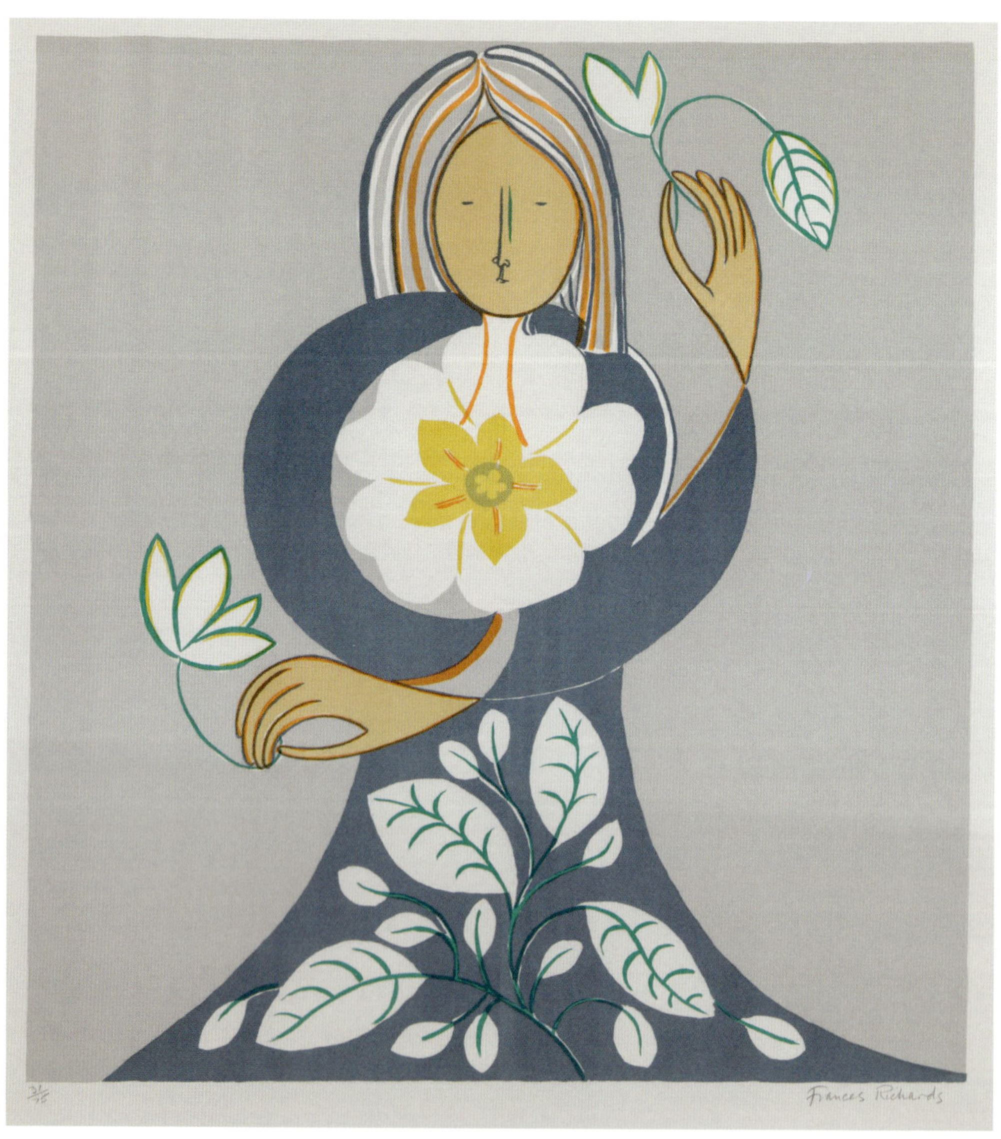

Hieratic Floral Figure, 1974, signed and numbered,
lithograph on paper, signed and numbered, 20 × 22 ¾ in. (51 cm × 58 cm).

Frances Richards (1903-1985)

Frances Richards was a multi-talented artist working variously as a painter, draughtswoman, fresco artist, potter, embroiderer, sculptor, teacher and poet. Soon after completing her scholarship at the Royal College of Art in 1930, Richards received her first professional commission when Stanley Morison, the founder of the Monotype Corporation, asked her to provide a series of lithographs inspired by The Twelve Acts of the Apostles. With their clean and delicate lines and touching evocation of mood and atmosphere, these early works are characteristic of the simple lyricism that would define Richard's graphic art and would still be in evidence half a century later in compositions such as *Hieratic Floral Figure*.

Throughout her life Richards' had a deep love of poetry and was particularly affected by the visionary symbolism of Arthur Rimbaud. The year after producing *Hieratic Floral Figure* she executed a set of lithographs, published by the Curwen Press, inspired by Rimbaud's *Les Illuminations* which were first published in 1886. Depicting figures in dream-like landscapes, the illustrations reveal the artist's love of early Renaissance painting, in particular the work of Fra Angelico.

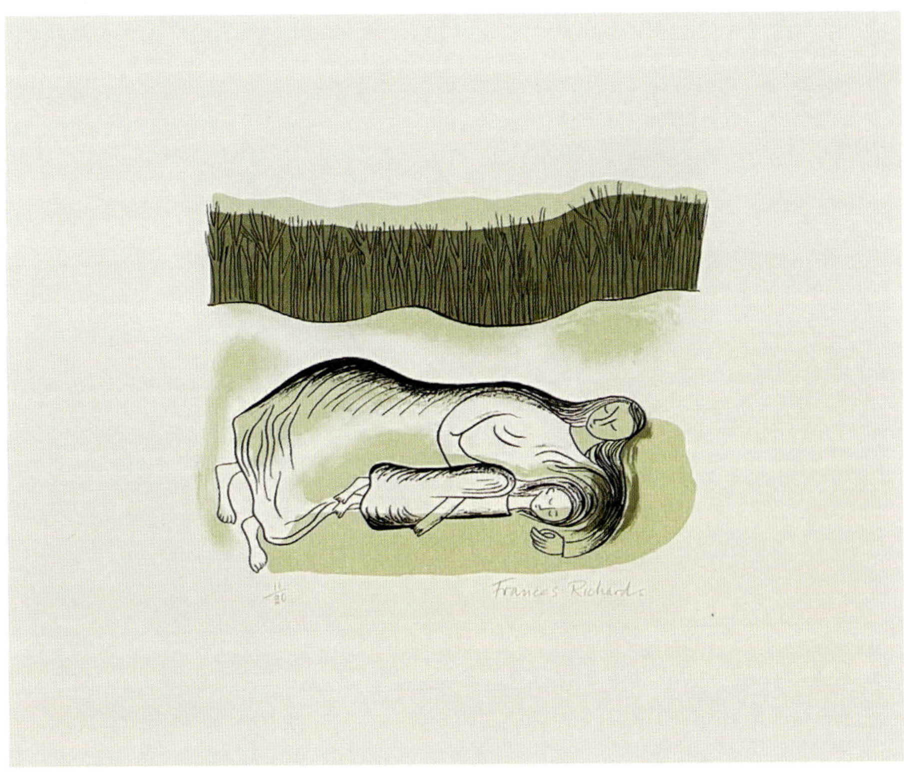

Dawn, from *Les Illuminations* - illustrations to prose poems by Arthur Rimbaud, 1973-75, lithograph on paper, signed and numbered, 6 ¼ x 8 ¼ in. (16.2 x 20.8 cm).

List of Abbreviations Used

Artists' International Association – AIA
Fine Art Society – FAS
International Society of Sculptors, Painters & Gravers – ISSPG
London Artists' Association – LAA
National Portrait Gallery – NPG
National Society of Painters, Sculptors and Printmakers – NS
New English Art Club – NEAC
Royal Academy – RA
Royal British Society of Sculptors – RBS
Royal College of Art – RCA
Royal Scottish Academy – RSA
Royal Society of British Artists – RBA
Royal Society of Painter-Printmakers – RE
Royal Society of Portrait Painters – RP
Royal Watercolour Society – RWS
Society of Women Artists – SWA
Society of Wood Engravers – SWE
Women's International Art Club – WIAC
World War I – WWI
World War II – WWII
London Group – LG

Marion Adnams (1898-1995)

Marion Adnams initially trained as a modern languages teacher; however, woodcuts she made while travelling in Europe during the 1920s received significant praise when she exhibited them at Derby Art Gallery, prompting her to re-train at Derby School of Art during the 1930s. She qualified as an art teacher in 1938 and in 1946 she became Head of Art at Derby Diocesan Training College.

From the late 1930s onwards, Adnams became known for her distinctive Surrealist paintings, and exhibited in local galleries and in London, including at the British Art Centre and the Modern Art Gallery. Although she never formally joined any Surrealist societies, she made a significant contribution to the movement, particularly regarding female/male dichotomies within the group, which she explored extensively in her work. In 2017 she was the subject of a retrospective at Derby Art Gallery.

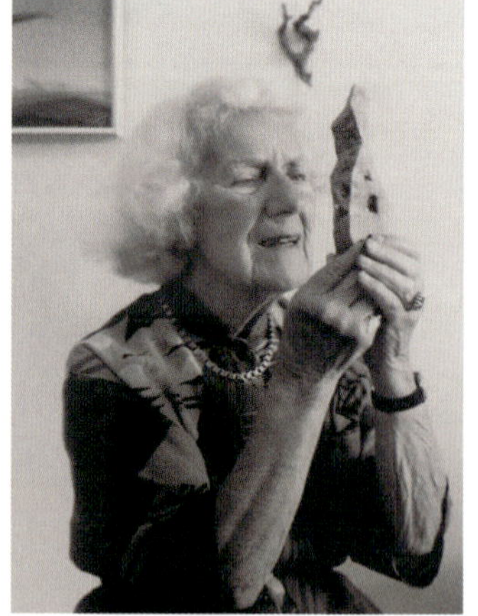

BIOGRAPHIES

Mary Adshead (1904-1995)

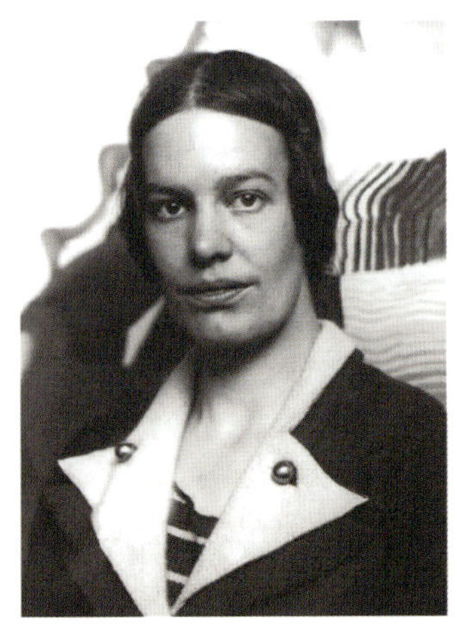

Mary Adshead studied at the Slade School of Fine Art (1920-24) under Henry Tonks (1862-1937), who in 1924 selected her for a mural commission at Highways boys' club in Shadwell, working with Rex Whistler (1905-1944). She became a prominent muralist, creating decorations for both public and private spaces, including the British Pavilion at the 1937 Paris International Exhibition. She also illustrated several books, such as *The Little Boy and His House* by Stephen Bone (1904-1958), whom she married in 1929, and made designs for London Transport and the Post Office.

As a noteworthy female artist, Adshead exhibited frequently at the WIAC from the mid-1930s, before serving on its committee in 1951. Working at a time when expectations of women were still largely confined to issues of domesticity, her prodigious professional output was noteworthy. Her approach to mural painting – especially in her choice of subjects and her colourful palette – challeged the perceived divisions which determined that public and private spaces should necessarily be treated differently. She was the subject of a retrospective at Liverpool Art Gallery in 2005.

Vanessa Bell (1879-1961)

Vanessa Bell (née Stephen) took drawing lessons from Ebenezer Cook before attending Sir Arthur Cope's art school in 1896 and the RA Schools (1901-04) under the tutelage of John Singer Sargent, amongst others.

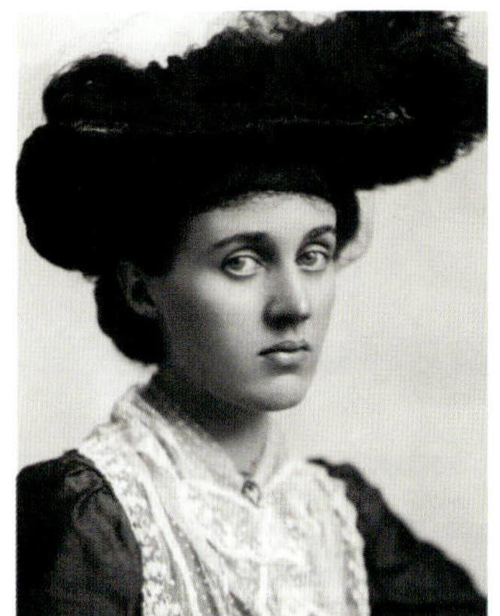

Following the death of her parents, Bell and her siblings moved from their family home to Bloomsbury, where they began socialising with the artists and writers that would eventually form the renowned Bloomsbury Group. In 1907 she married fellow Bloomsbury member Clive Bell.

During this time, Bell began to embrace artistic experimentation. With Roger Fry and Duncan Grant she co-founded the Omega Workshops, an artists' co-operative for decorative arts that operated between 1913 and 1919. Throughout the 1920s and 1930s, she worked in collaboration with Grant and alone on numerous interior decorative schemes, designing rugs, furnishings and murals. She also exhibited with the LG and with the LAA after its founding in 1925. In 2017, her work was the subject of a major retrospective at Dulwich Picture Gallery.

Hilda Carline (1889 -1950)

Hilda Carline studied at Percyval Tudor-Hart's School of Painting in Hampstead (1913) and served with the Women's Land Army (1916-18), before enrolling at the Slade School of Fine Art under Henry Tonks in 1918. Quickly gaining critical recognition, she exhibited at the LG (1921), the RA and the NEAC. This impressive start to her career faltered, particularly after she married, in 1925, the artist Stanley Spencer (1891-1959). Their turbulent union resulted in periods when Carline hardly painted at all and eventually, in 1942, she suffered a breakdown.

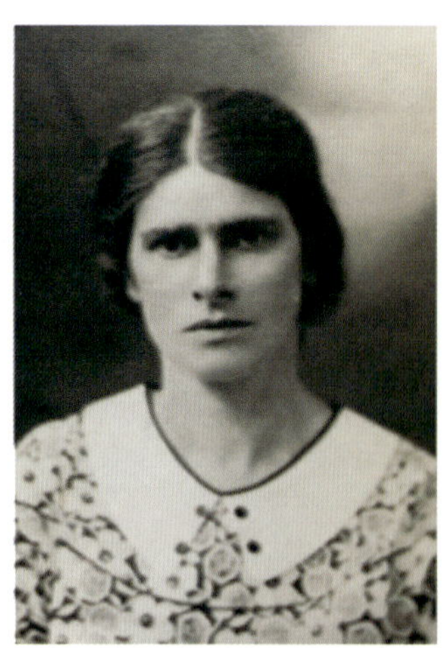

Nevertheless, she never neglected painting entirely, and even during these challenging times produced animated, vigorous work, such as her 1933 portrait of Patricia Preece (1894-1966) – her husband's mistress – entitled *Lady in Green*.

After her divorce in 1937, Carline began working more frequently once again, producing numerous pastels which explored her religious beliefs.

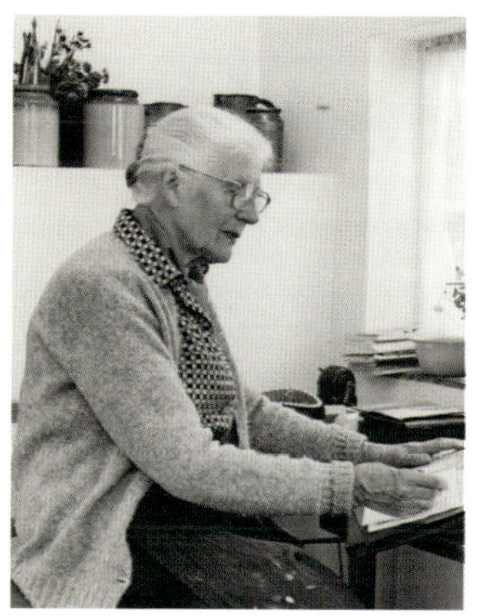

Jean Clark (1902-1999)

Born in Sidcup, Kent, Jean Clark studied at Sidcup School of Art under C. Ross Burnett and at the RA Schools under Charles Sims and Ernest Jackson, before attending the Académie Julian in Paris. She married fellow artist John Cosmo Clark in 1924, and together they travelled to America, where they worked and exhibited. In the 1930s, she took a post at a small art school run by Walter Sickert in Broadstairs, Kent. As a painter and muralist, her commissions included murals at Cutlers' Hall, Sheffield and Corpus Christi Church in Weston-super-Mare. She also painted a ceiling for Woodford Green United Free Church in Essex. She exhibited at the RA, RBA, RP, RWA, and NEAC who elected her a member in 1952, and in 1972 she was elected a member of RWS and the Art Workers' Guild. A joint retrospective of her work with Cosmo was held at Bankside Gallery in London in 1983, and Chappel Galleries held another joint Jean and Cosmo Clark show in 2002.

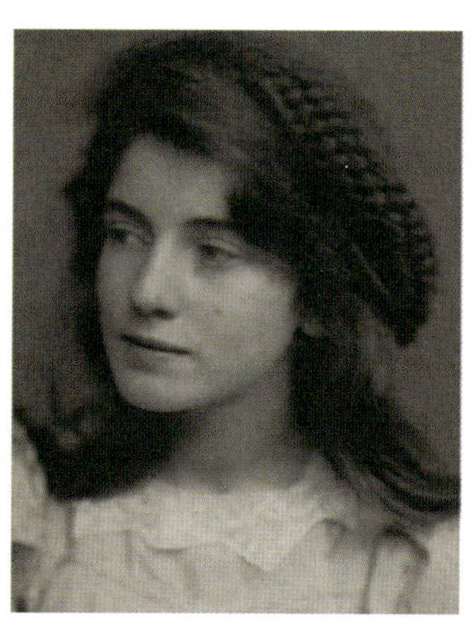

Edna Clarke Hall (1879-1979)

Edna Clarke Hall (née Edna Waugh) studied at the Slade School of Fine Art (1895-99). Here, she was taught by the renowned artist, Henry Tonks, and won several awards, including a scholarship in 1897. She developed an affinity for working in watercolour whilst studying at the institution.

Edna began to exhibit less often following her early marriage in 1898 to William Clarke Hall, a man thirteen years her senior. The marital difficulties experienced by Edna, driven by her conflicting desire to pursue an artistic career in contrast to William's wish that she concentrated on wifely duties, are well documented. In 1914 she held a solo show at the Chenil Galleries in London; five years later, however, she suffered a nervous breakdown. From 1922 she began to exhibit again following therapy. Edna was also a poet and had several volumes published in the 1920s and 1930s. She became a Lady in 1932 due to the recognition of her husband's work in reforming child law.

Ithell Colquhoun (1906-1988)

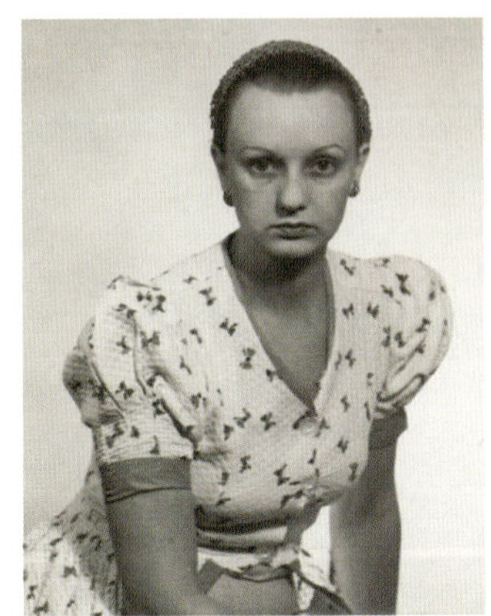

Ithell Colquhoun studied at Cheltenham Art School (1925-7) and the Slade School of Fine Art (1927-31), winning joint first prize with Elizabeth Leslie Arnold (1909-2005) in the 1929 Summer Composition Competition.

She discovered Surrealism in Paris in 1932, held her first solo exhibition at Cheltenham Art Gallery in 1936 and in 1939 joined the British Surrealist Group. She was particularly interested in automatic painting and how it could unlock not just the unconscious mind but also the mystical.

Despite her expulsion from the English Surrealist Group in 1940 due to her increasing preoccupation with the occult, Colquhoun remained active in Surrealist circles – she was married to Toni del Renzio from 1943-48. She wrote and illustrated numerous books, including *The Living Stones: Cornwall* (1957), and exhibited at the Leicester Galleries and with the LG and WIAC. She took part in several Surrealist retrospectives in the 1970s, including a solo show at the Newlyn Gallery in 1976, and the terms of her will bequeathed her studio (over 3000 works) to the National Trust who transferred it to Tate in 2020.

Catherine Dawson Giles (1878-1955)

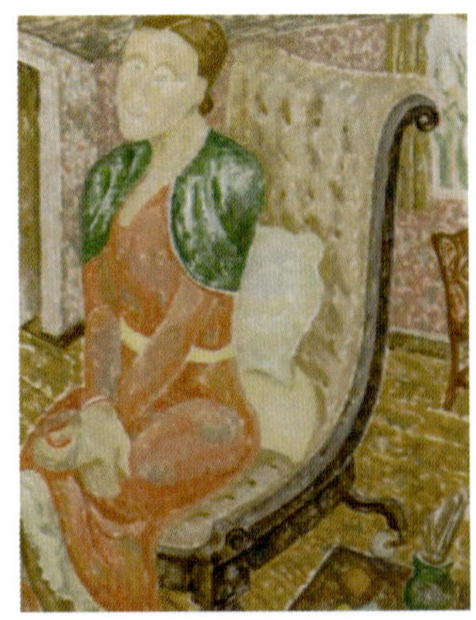

Catherine Dawson Giles
by Jessica Dismorr (1885-1939).

Born in Lewisham in South East London, Catherine Dawson Giles studied at Goldsmiths College in 1900 before furthering her art education at the RA Schools and later under Max Bohm in Étaples, France. Here, she met and became a lifelong friend of Jessica Dismorr, with whom she worked and travelled frequently. Indeed, Giles travelled extensively throughout Europe and Northern Africa during the 1920s and 1930s on painting trips, and – after working as a nurse in London during WWI – again in Italy between the wars.

Elected member of the Society of Painters in Tempera, she exhibited with the ISSPG, LG, and NEAC, and she also had a solo show at the Claridge Galleries. She continued painting into the 1950s, and was the subject of a retrospective alongside Dismorr in 2000 at the FAS.

Valentine Dobrée (1894-1974)

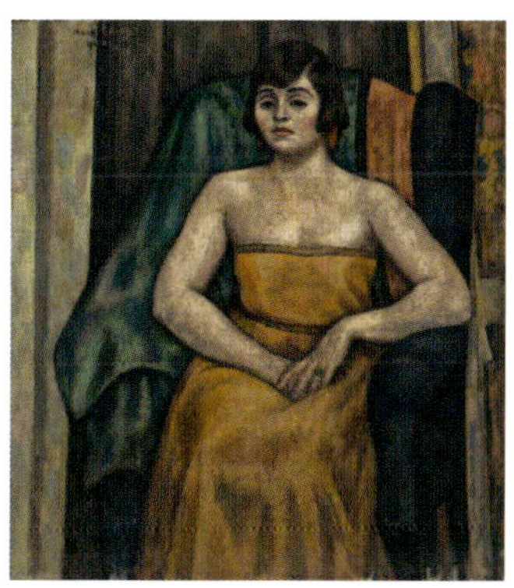

Valentine Dobrée, 1919,
by Mark Gertler (1891-1939).

Valentine Dobrée (née Gladys May Mabel Brooke-Pechell) emigrated to England from India at the age of three. Despite brief tutelage from André Derain (1880-1954) being her only formal art education, she enjoyed a successful career as an artist, novelist and poet. She married in 1913 and moved with her husband to Florence, returning to England at the beginning of the war where she lived a bohemian existence – becoming associated with the Bloomsbury group and conducting an affair with Mark Gertler.

Dobrée showed with the LG in 1920 and at the *Salon des Indépendants* between 1921 and 1925, while living in the French Pyrenees with her husband. In 1926 they moved to Cairo, returning to England in 1929 when her book *The Emperor's Tigers* was published. She held her first solo show at the Claridge Gallery in 1931, and the Institute of Contemporary Arts staged an exhibition of her collages in 1963. The Stanley and Audrey Burton Gallery, Leeds, held a retrospective exhibition in 2000.

Phyllis Dodd (1899-1995)

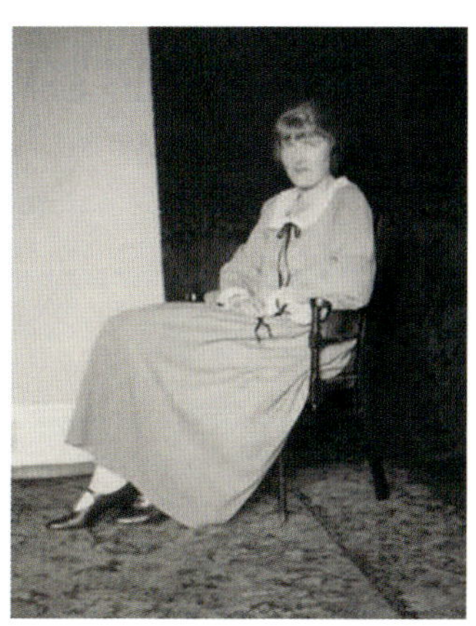

Phyllis Dodd achieved considerable success from early on in her prolific career. Studying at the Liverpool School of Art from 1917-21, she received a Royal Exhibition Scholarship and attended the Royal College of Art for four years – alongside Henry Moore (1898-1986), Raymond Coxon (1896-1997) and Edna Ginesi (1902-2000), winning the Drawing Prize in her final year.

From 1925 to 1930 she taught part-time at Walthamstow Technical College. In 1928, she married the artist Douglas Percy Bliss (1900-1984) and they worked alongside each other, exhibiting together at Derby Art Gallery in 1947. She also exhibited at the NEAC, the RA, the RP, the Walker Art Gallery and the RSA, and in 1989 the Hatton Gallery at Newcastle University held a large retrospective exhibition to celebrate her ninetieth birthday.

Evelyn Dunbar (1906 -1960)

Evelyn Dunbar, a committed Christian Scientist, studied at Rochester School of Art, Chelsea School of Art (1927) and the Royal College of Art (1929-1933). She painted murals from 1933-1936 at Brockley School, a collaboration with her RCA tutor (and lover until 1937) Cyril 'Charles' Mahoney, with whom she wrote and illustrated the revolutionary *Gardeners' Choice*. In 1940 she was appointed a war artist, the only woman (among 36 men) to be employed full-time by the WAAC. Her recording of women's home front activities also enabled her to promote a subtle feminism.

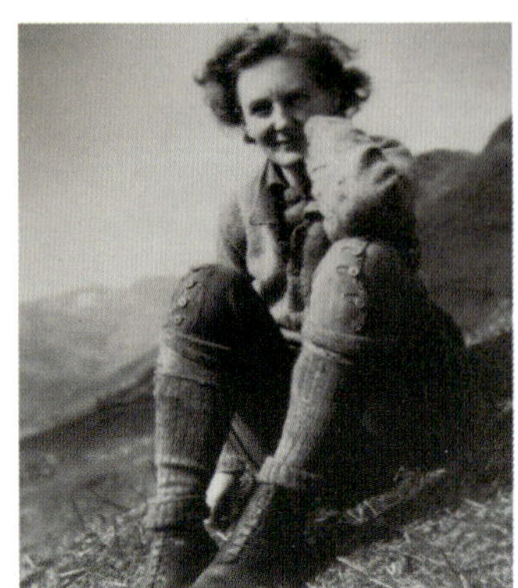

Primarily an illustrator, Dunbar's post-war period, continued her promotion of women's interests through allegory and narrative painting. She held her only solo exhibition at Wye, Kent, in 1953, although the WAAC included numerous pieces in touring exhibitions on both sides of the Atlantic. Largely forgotten after her death at the age of 53, interest in her work was rekindled with a posthumous exhibition at Lymington in 2006. In 2015 Liss Llewellyn mounted a major retrospective exhibition of her recently rediscovered studio at Pallant House Gallery, Chichester.

Margaret Duncan (1906-1979)

Margaret L. Duncan worked as an art teacher at Huyton College School from 1935 to 1947 before moving to St Katherine's College in Tottenham; she retained a close association with Huyton throughout her life.

A diligent and committed teacher, she made precise watercolour landscapes and discerning humorous drawings that demonstrated her concern for simple authenticity. Her painting *The Annunciation* was exhibited at the RA in 1941.

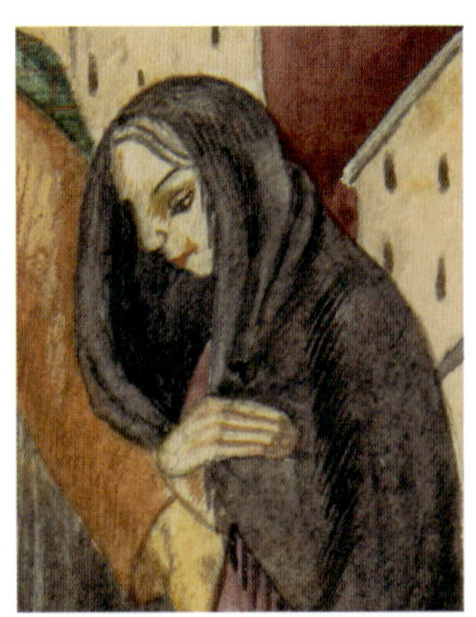

Annie French (1872-1965)

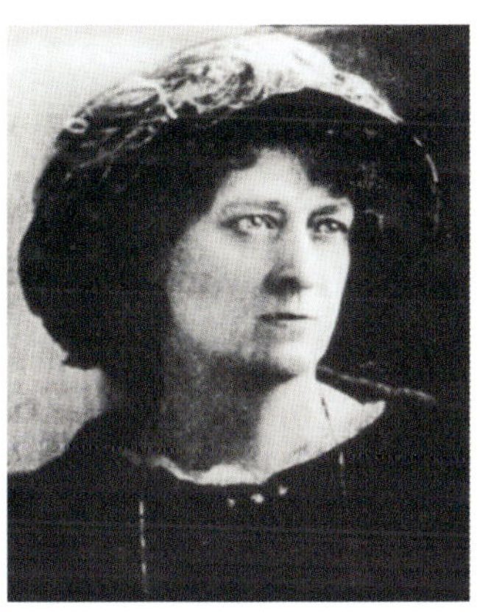

Annie French studied at the Glasgow School of Art (1886-89) where she was taught by the renowned teacher Francis Newberry. Here, she developed her technique of line drawing and an affinity for romantic subjects. French became known for creating small-scale Art Nouveau-inspired works. She subsequently taught ceramic decoration at the School from 1908 to 1912. In 1914, French relocated to London after her marriage to fellow artist, George Woolliscroft Rhead, in the same year.

From 1903 until 1924, French exhibited her works in galleries including the RA in London, the Royal Scottish Academy, and the Royal Glasgow Institute of the Fine Arts. Part of the Glasgow School, French was associated with the 'Glasgow Girls' group of artists. The Glasgow School promoted the idea that art and design should be an integral part of daily life, as opposed to the historical and neo-classical fine art revered by the Academy.

Tirzah Garwood (1908-1951)

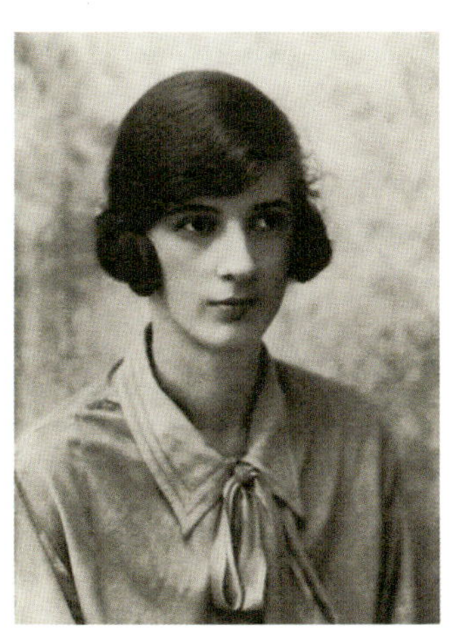

Eileen 'Tirzah' Garwood attended Eastbourne School of Art (1925-28), where she was taught by Eric Ravilious (1903-1942) whom she married in 1930.

She first exhibited in 1927, at the Redfern Gallery, and an early woodcut shown at the 1927 SWE exhibition received significant praise in The Times. Such was the originality of her printmaking that she exerted an influence over Ravilious' own wood engravings. She was also commissioned by the BBC in 1928 to illustrate Granville Bantock's *The Pilgrim's Progress*, and made whimsical but exacting observational pictures that were popular with children and exhibited by the Society for Education in Art.

While recovering from emergency mastectomy surgery in 1942 she wrote her autobiography, *Long Live Great Bardfield & Love to You All* (published posthumously in 2012). After Ravilious' death that same year, Garwood remained in Essex until her remarriage in 1946. She was again diagnosed with cancer in 1948 and died in 1951. In 1952, a memorial exhibition was held at the Towner Gallery in Eastbourne.

Evelyn Gibbs (1905-1991)

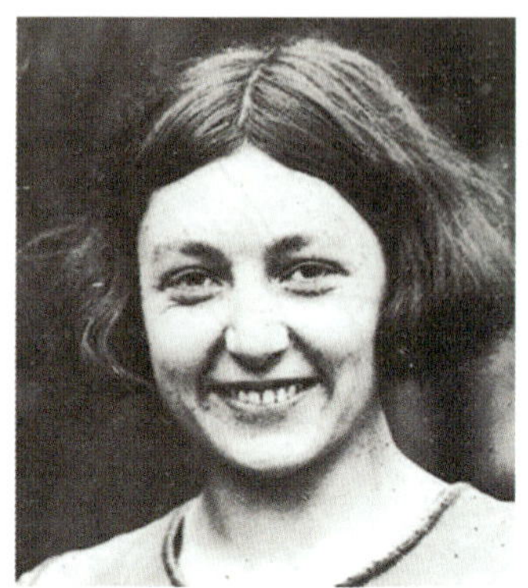

Evelyn Gibbs studied at the Liverpool School of Art (1922-26) and at the RCA (1926-29). Credited with making significant gains for women in art and academia, she was the second woman to win the Prix de Rome for Engraving (1929) and was elected an associate of the RE in the same year.

In London, after returning from Rome in 1931, she taught at a school for handicapped children and later wrote *The Teaching of Art in Schools*, which was published in 1934 – the same year she was appointed lecturer at Goldsmiths College.

She founded the Midland Group of Artists in 1943 after Goldsmiths was evacuated to Nottingham, and in that September was commissioned as an official war artist to record 'Women making munitions' while working in Blood Transfusion and in the Women's Voluntary Service. Seven of the works made during this time are held in the Imperial War Museum in London. In 1945 she married Hugh Willatt, later Secretary-General of the Arts Council.

Phyllis Ginger (1907-2005)

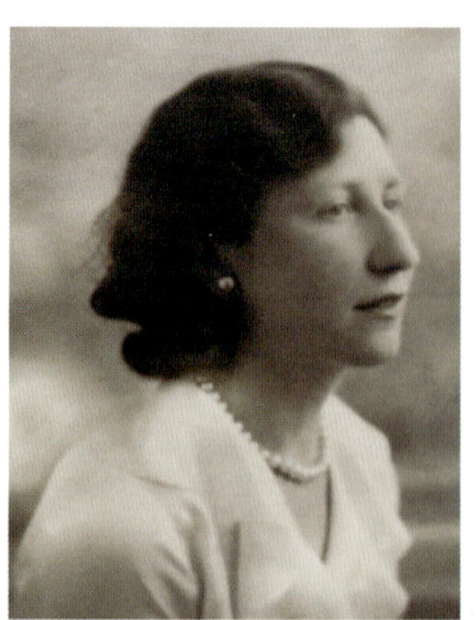

Phyllis Ethel Ginger was born in New Malden, Surrey. She studied at the Tiffin Girls' School, Kingston upon Thames, attending evening classes at the nearby Kingston School of Art. From 1932–35, she studied at Richmond School of Art under Stanley Badmin and attended evening classes at the Central School of Arts and crafts under WP Robins, before winning a scholarship aged 30 to become a full-time student there under John Farleigh and Clarke Hutton.

Although her primary ambition had been to become an illustrator, her interest in etching and portraiture was encouraged by her tutors. She was a prolific book illustrator and designer of graphic advertisements and book covers. In the years immediately following WWII, her work was reproduced in the Pictures for Schools series, and she designed and illustrated numerous book-jackets and books during the 1950s.

Throughout her career, she exhibited regularly with the RWS (of which she became a member in 1958), as well as with the RA and NEAC. She also joined the AIA.

Edith Granger-Taylor (1887-1958)

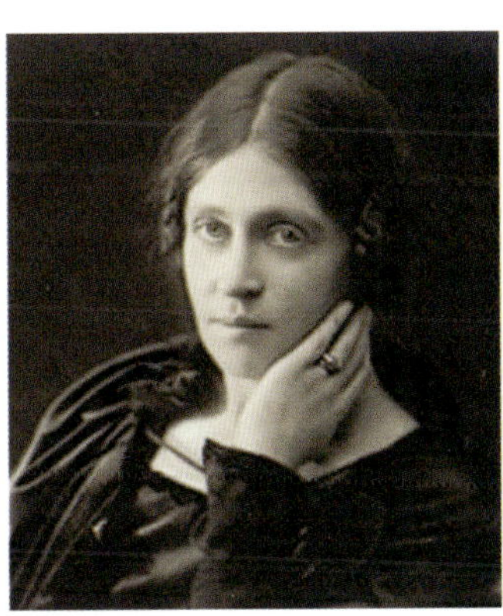

Edith Granger-Taylor began painting as a child, attending the Royal Academy Schools (1910), St. John's Wood Art School, and the Slade School of Fine Art for a term in 1919, where she studied under Henry Tonks. She also returned to the Slade in the early 1930s to study stage design.

She exhibited numerously in the 1920s and 1930s, including at the NEAC, the RE exhibition in 1935, and with solo shows at the Grosvenor Galleries (1922) and Beaux Arts Gallery (1932). However, her increasing frustration as a female artist working in the inter-war years, showcased in paintings such as *Allegory* (1934) (which she referred to as a "delicate feminist satire"), caused her to retreat from the art world, and after the 1930s her work would not be exhibited again in her lifetime.

Kathleen Guthrie (1905-1981)

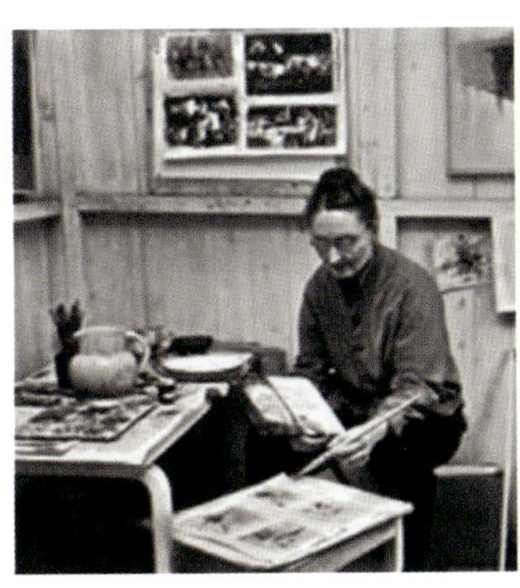

Kathleen Hilda Guthrie (née Maltby) was born in Feltham, Middlesex. She studied at the Slade School of Fine Art under Henry Tonks (1922–24) and later at the RCA (1925). While at the Slade, she met Robin Guthrie, a fellow student, and they married in 1927, before moving in 1931 to America, where he was appointed director of the School of Fine Art in Boston. Kathleen was given her first solo show at the Grace Horne Gallery in 1932, exhibiting New England landscapes and narrative scenes painted in her signature whimsical figurative style.

From the 1930s onwards she exhibited widely, especially at the NEAC and the RA. She also showed with the Whitechapel Art Gallery, Loggia Gallery, AIA and at the WIAC. In 1941, following the breakdown of her first marriage, she married Cecil Stephenson, and from this point on her work became increasingly abstract. In the mid-1960s, she began producing silkscreen prints and became established as one of the most prominent practitioners of her generation.

Gertrude Hermes (1901-1983)

Gertrude Hermes attended the Beckenham School of Art (c.1921) and the Brook Green School of Painting and Sculpture (1922), where she met Blair Hughes-Stanton (1902-1981), whom she married in 1926. Although they divorced in 1933, they collaborated on several projects, including wood engravings for *The Pilgrim's Progress*, published in 1928. She also collaborated with her friends Naomi Mitchison and Prunella Clough (1919-1999) to explore depictions of feminine desire.

The 1930s were a prosperous decade for Hermes, who exhibited for the first time at the Redfern Gallery in 1932. She also showed regularly at the RA from 1934, was elected a member of the LG in 1935, and in 1939 represented Britain at the Venice Biennale.

In the late 1940s to early 1950s, she taught at the Central School of Art, and became the first woman engraver to be elected a full member of the RA in 1971 – eventually receiving an OBE in 1981.

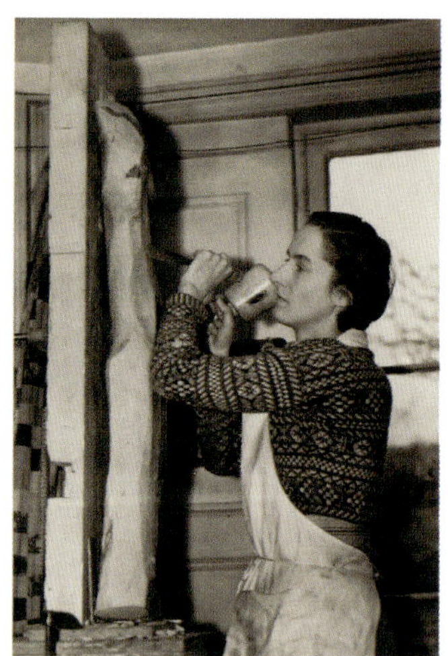

Gladys Hynes (1888-1958)

Gladys Hynes was born in Indore, India, to an Irish Catholic family, with whom she emigrated to London in 1891, later studying at the London School of Art in Earl's Court. After her family moved to Penzance in 1906, she attended the Stanhope Forbes School of Painting, Newlyn, She returned to London in 1919, where she settled in Hampstead.

Hynes was a supporter of the Irish Republican cause. A member of the CWSS, she was also an impassioned campaigner for women's rights, often challenging the social construction of gender and sexuality in her work. Many of the paintings she produced during WWII were shaped by her mainly pacifist convictions.

During her career, Hynes contributed to Roger Fry's (1866-1934) Omega Workshops, illustrated books – including the folio edition of Ezra Pound's *A Draft of the Cantos* nos. XVII to XXVII (1928) – undertook sculpture commissions and theatre designs. She exhibited with the RA, the LG, the International Society of Sculptors, the Paris Salon and at the 1924 Venice Biennale.

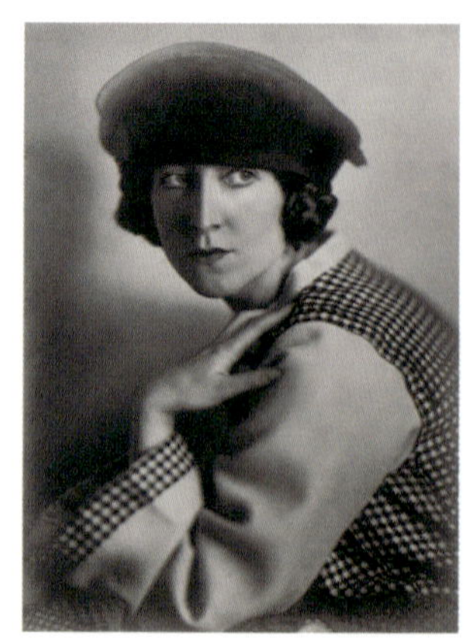

Frances Hodgkins (1869-1947)

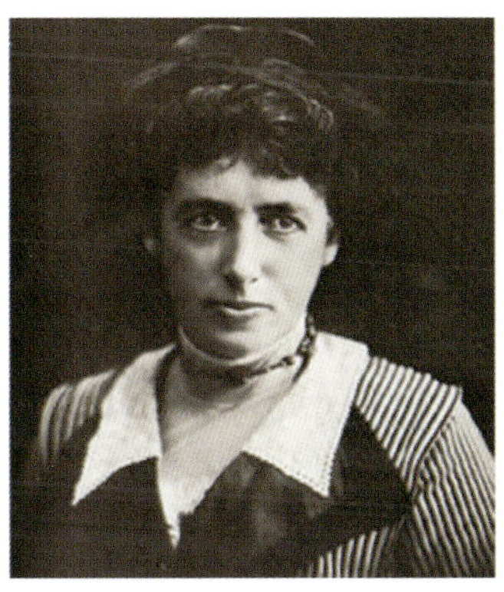

Frances Hodgkins studied at the Dunedin School of Art and Design, New Zealand. She primarily produced landscape and still life paintings, but also designed textiles. She is renowned for her modernist style, inspired by the Impressionist, Post-Impressionist, and Fauvist exhibitions of the time. Hodgkins first exhibited her work in 1887 with the Otago Art Society in New Zealand.

Despite growing up in New Zealand, Hodgkins spent much of her life in Europe. She first visited London in 1901, where she studied at the City of London Polytechnic. Subsequently, she travelled to Paris and Italy. Hodgkins portrayed her origins when she exhibited at the *Colonial Art Exhibition* (1902) in London, contributing works which depicted the streets of Dinan, New Zealand. She later exhibited at a diverse array of galleries, including the RA and the Fine Art Society in London. In 1929, Hodgkins was invited to join the avant-garde 7&5 group of artists while living in St Ives, Cornwall. The Lefevre Gallery held a retrospective exhibition of her career in 1946.

Julia Beatrice How (1867-1932)

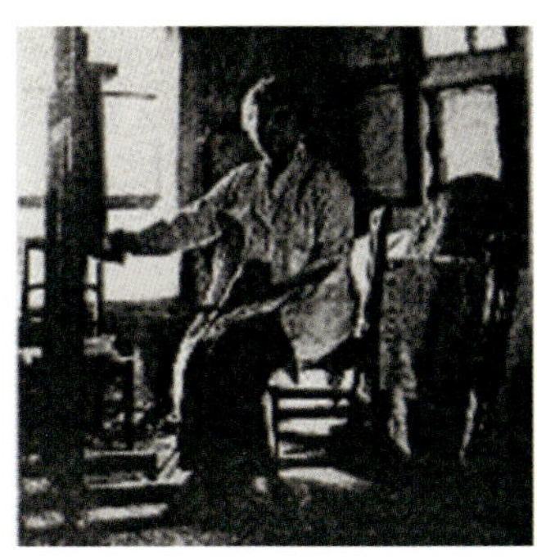

Julia Beatrice How was born in Devon, England, but later worked in Paris following her acceptance into the prestigious Académie Delécluse around the year 1893. She exhibited her work first in 1902 at the Société Nationale des Beaux-Arts. How spent most of her life in France and established a workshop in Étaples. She exhibited extensively in Paris, including at the Salon des Tuileries (1923-24). How enjoyed further success in England through the exhibition of two paintings at the Royal Academy, along with a posthumous work in 1936. In London, she also exhibited at several other galleries, such as the Beaux Arts Gallery (1927) and the Fine Art Society (1987); the former, along with the New Burlington Galleries, held memorial exhibitions in her honour in 1933 and 1935 respectively.

How worked with a variety of media, including crayons, oils, and watercolours. After 1910, she concentrated on studies of women and children in interiors for which she has become best-known. Her ability to utilise tone to create an almost transparent effect in her paintings has attracted much critical success

Barbara Jones (1912-1978)

Barbara Jones first attended art school in Croydon (1931-33) before winning a scholarship to the RCA (1933-36), where she met painter Cliff Barry whom she married in 1941.

A prolific and varied artist, during WWII she worked with the Pilgrim Trust on the Recording Britain series, making one of the largest contributions of the 63 artists taking part. She wrote and illustrated books on design history, many of which are today considered seminal, including *The Unsophisticated Arts*, 1951 and *Design for Death*, 1967.

In 1951, she organised the *Black Eyes and Lemonade: Curating Popular Art* exhibition held at the Whitechapel Gallery for the Festival of Britain. A fellow of the Society of Industrial Artists from the same year, she was made vice president in 1969. She was also a fellow of the Royal Anthropological Institute and a member of the Society of Authors. A retrospective exhibition of the contents of her studio was held at Katharine House Gallery, Marlborough, in 1999.

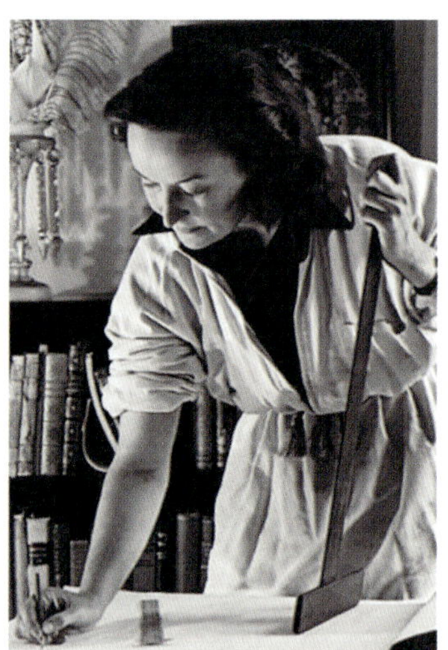

Lucy Kemp-Welch (1869-1958)

Lucy Kemp-Welch first exhibited at the age of fourteen. Raised in Bournemouth, she studied at a local art school before subsequently enrolling at Hubert von Herkomer's art school in Bushey in 1891. Welch enjoyed much success at the latter institution, and later progressed to run the school from 1905 until 1926.

Kemp-Welch is primarily known for her animal paintings. During her childhood, she sketched ponies in the New Forest. One of her horse paintings, *Colt-Hunting in the New Forest* (1897), was purchased by the Tate after being exhibited at the RA. She later illustrated Anna Sewell's novel, *Black Beauty*, in 1915. During World War One, she was commissioned to produce an artwork for the army recruitment poster, *Forward! Forward to Victory Enlist Now* (1914). Kemp-Welch received critical acclaim for her works during her lifetime. She became one of the first two female members of the RBA in England. Her talent at depicting animals was also recognised when she was awarded medals by the Paris Salon.

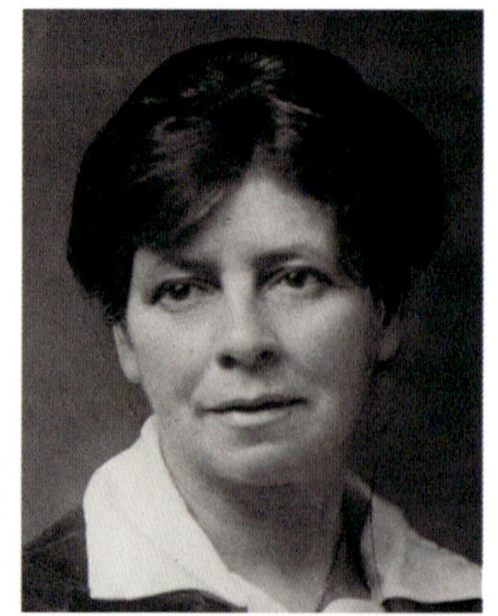

Winifred Knights (1899 -1947)

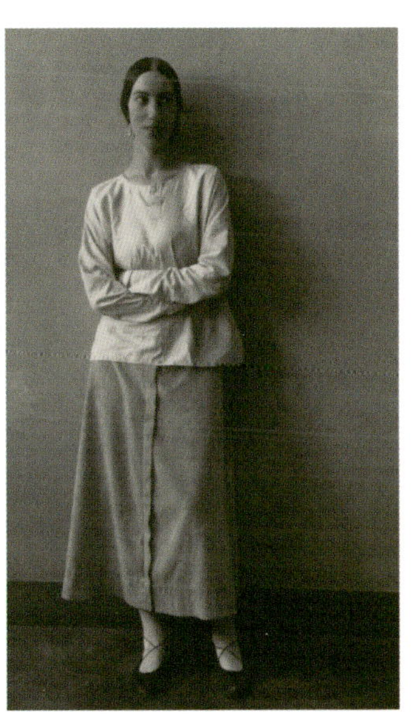

Winifred Knights was born in Streatham, London in 1899. She studied at the Slade School of Fine Art (1915-17, 1918-20 and 1926-27). In 1919 she jointly won the Slade Summer Composition Competition with *A Scene in a Village Street with Mill-Hands Conversing*. In 1920, she became the first woman to win the Scholarship in Decorative Painting awarded by the British School at Rome. She remained in Italy until December 1925, marrying fellow Rome Scholar Thomas Monnington (1902-1976) in April 1924. On her return to England, Knights received a commission to paint an altarpiece for the Milner Memorial Chapel in Canterbury. A major commission for the Earl of Crawford and Balcarres, on which she had been working for five years, remained unconcluded at her early death, aged 47.

Throughout her life, Winifred Knights produced work through which she explored women's autonomy. Presenting herself as the central protagonist, and selecting models from her inner circle, she rewrote and reinterpreted fairy tale and legend, biblical narrative and pagan mythology. She was the subject of a retrospective exhibition at Dulwich Picture Gallery in 2016.

Clare Leighton (1898-1989)

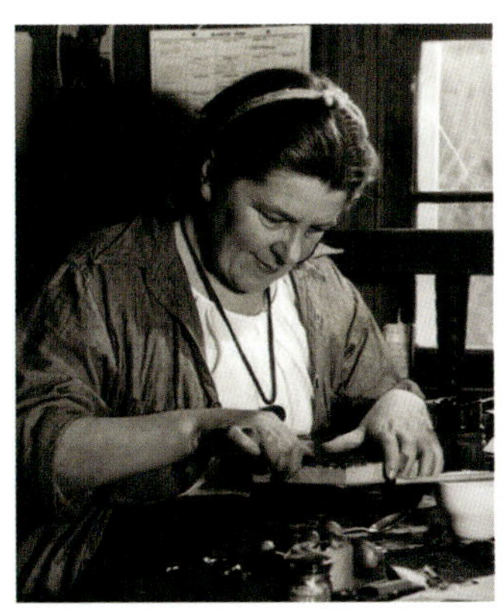

Clare Leighton attended the Brighton School of Art (1915), the Slade School of Fine Art (1921-23) and the Central School of Arts and Crafts. Despite her childhood nickname 'The Bystander', she became a hugely visible artist on both sides of the Atlantic, and her vast oeuvre includes engravings, paintings, bookplates, illustrations and stained glass. Her twelve plates for Wedgewood, New England Industries, 1952, are amongst her best-known work.

She exhibited with the SWE in London (1923) and at the 1934 Venice Biennale – attaining full membership to the Royal Society of Painter-Etchers and Engravers in the same year. She also made several tours of the United States, becoming a naturalised citizen in 1945. By the time of her death, Leighton had authored twelve books and made over 840 prints.

Thérèse Lessore (1884-1945)

Thérèse Lessore studied at the South-Western Polytechnic Art School, followed by the Slade School of Fine Art. Whilst attending the Slade (1904-9), she won the Melville Nettleship Prize for Figure Composition. Later, she founded the London Group with her first husband Bernard Adeney in 1913. The London Group brought together members of the Camden Town Group and the Vorticists. Lessore exhibited regularly with the group. An art critic for the *Daily Herald* described her contribution to a group exhibition as 'really original work'.

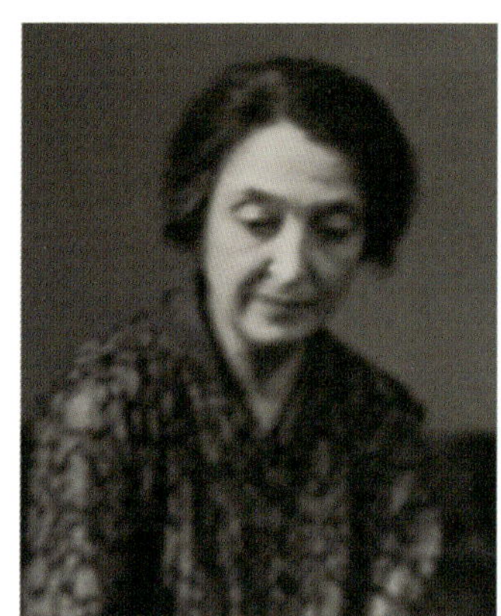

Lessore had her first solo exhibition in 1918 at the Eldar Gallery, London. The catalogue for the exhibition was written by her second husband, the Camden Town artist Walter Sickert, whom she married in 1926. Together, they shared a love of popular entertainment and they frequently visited music halls and circuses for artistic inspiration. Many of her artworks reflect this fascination. Lessore worked primarily in oil and watercolour, although she also produced etchings and designed pottery for Wedgwood.

Dorothy Mahoney (1902-1984)

Dorothy Louise Mahoney (née Bishop) was born in Wednesbury, Staffordshire, and studied first at the Ryland School of Art in West Bromwich (1918-24), before obtaining a scholarship to attend the RCA in 1924, where she studied lettering and illumination under Edward Johnston. From 1927-8, she taught art and crafts in London County Council classes for women, and in 1928 she accepted a position to teach at Woolwich Polytechnic School of Art.

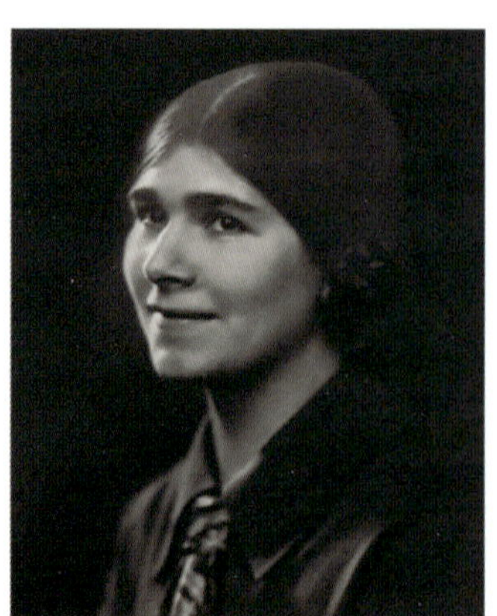

In 1939, she was appointed tutor in charge of calligraphy at the RCA, evacuating to Ambleside, Westmorland, with the college the next year. It was in Ambleside that she and her colleague Charles Mahoney were married. She gave birth to a daughter, Elizabeth, in 1944. After leaving the RCA in 1953, she taught at the Central School of Arts and Crafts and Ravensbourne School of Art.

She was elected a member of the Arts and Crafts Exhibition Society, Art Workers' Guild and the Society of Scribes and Illuminators. She exhibited frequently with the SSI, Society of Designer Craftsmen and SWA.

Gwenda Morgan (1908-1991)

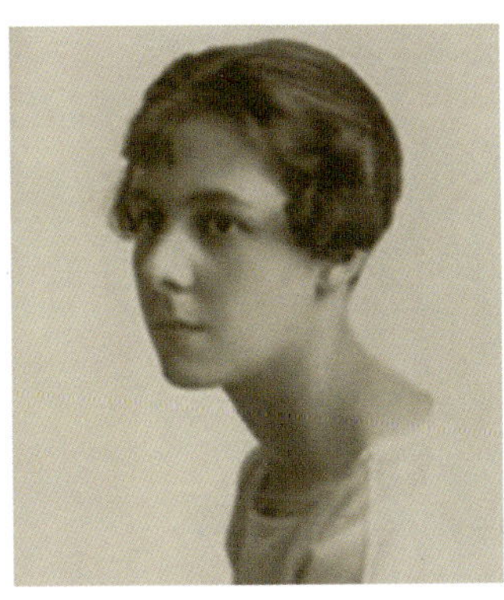

Gwenda Morgan was a British wood engraver born in Petworth. She studied at Goldsmiths' College of Art in London (1926-1930) and then attended the Grosvenor School of Modern Art in Pimlico. The Grosvenor School was a progressive art school with a democratic approach to the arts, reflected in its championing of wood engraving and linocuts.

Morgan illustrated a number of books published by private presses, the main body of her work drawing upon the landscape and buildings around Petworth and the neighbouring South Downs. Throughout the Second World War she worked as a Land Girl just outside Petworth. Her record of those years was published by the Whittington Press in 2002 as *The Diary of a Land Girl, 1939-1945*.

Her prints are held in the collections of the Victoria and Albert Museum and the British Museum in London, the Ashmolean Museum in Oxford, and the Fitzwilliam Museum in Cambridge, among others.

Anne Newland (1913-1997)

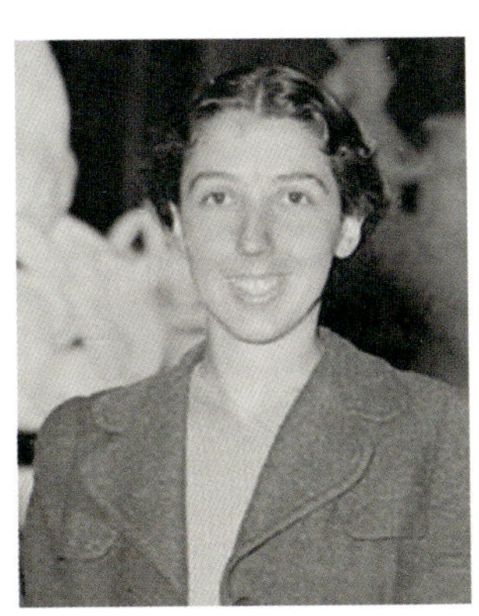

Anne Newland (1913-1997) was born in Wiltshire, and studied at the Byam Shaw School of Art (1936-38) under F Ernest Jackson. She was awarded an Abbey Major Scholarship in 1938 to study at the British School in Rome, and the following year received a full Rome Scholarship.

During WWII she worked for the Civil Defence Camouflage Establishment, and then taught in Scotland.

She was particularly influenced by the work of Italian Renaissance artists, especially Andrea Mantegna. The principal work she produced in Rome was a cartoon for a large mural of *The Legend of Ceres* that she envisioned as the central panel of a triptych – albeit one she never intended to produce. She returned to the idea a decade later, with a pencil drawing entitled *Composition, The Legend of Ceres* (dated 1949); in 1950 she exhibited at the RA with a variation on the theme entitled *Three Marys*. She also showed at the RSA and elsewhere during her lifetime.

Nancy Nicholson (1899 -1977)

Annie 'Nancy' Mary Pryde Nicholson was a painter and fabric designer, and the only daughter of esteemed artists Sir William Nicholson (1872-1949) and Mabel Pryde (1871-1918). She married the poet Robert Graves in 1918, although the relationship was not to last. She established Poulk Prints in 1929, and after a period of living with poet Geoffrey Taylor in the 1930s, she set up and collaborated with him on the Poulk Press. During this time, she also worked with her brother Ben (1894-1982) and his wife, the artist and sculptor Barbara Hepworth (1903-1975), on numerous textile designs.

A lifelong feminist, Nicholson promoted contraception while it was still illegal, often setting up stalls to provide information and support for women.

During the 1940s, she had a shop on Motcomb Street in London where she printed and displayed her fabrics, and her work was exhibited at the Victoria and Albert Museum in 1976.

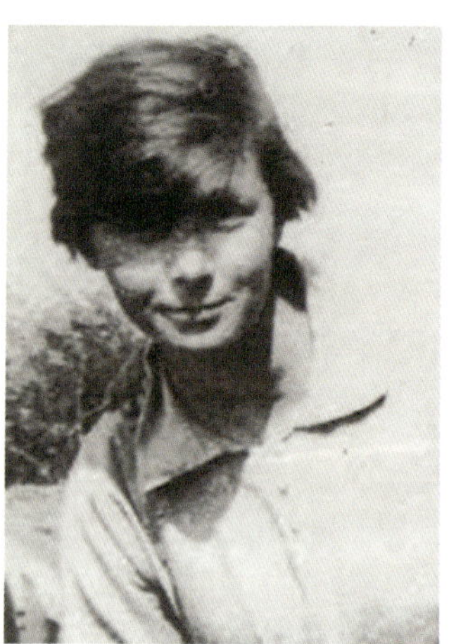

Muriel Pemberton (1909-1993)

Muriel Pemberton was a painter and teacher born in Tunstall, Stoke on Trent 8 September 1909. She invented art-school training in fashion in Britain and, in doing so, affected attitudes to fashion design throughout Europe. She brought the freedom of a painter to the discipline of designing and making clothes, and throughout her career she pursued in tandem her two great talents for painting and design.

As a result of her inspiration and initiative, Pemberton was awarded the first Diploma in Fashion by the RCA in 1931, and immediately began to teach fashion drawing two days a week at St Martin's School of Art. Pemberton's qualities as a painter, as distinct from those as a teacher, were revealed to many of her students only in retrospect, at an exhibition held in 1993 at Chris Beetles Gallery to coincide with the publication of her biography written by John Russell Taylor.

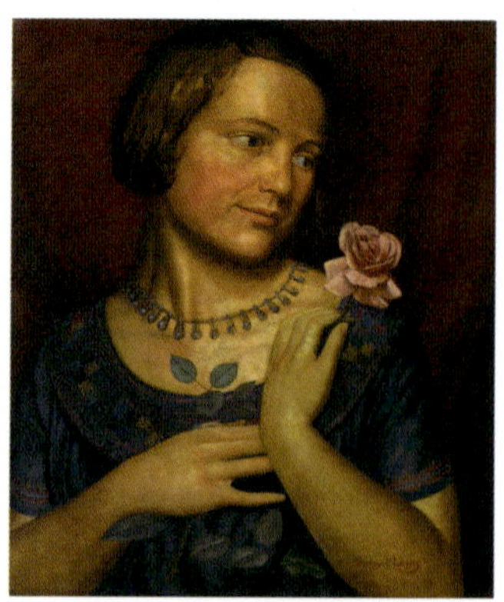

Muriel Pemberton, c.1929, by Stanley Lewis (1905-2009).

Gwen Raverat (1885-1957)

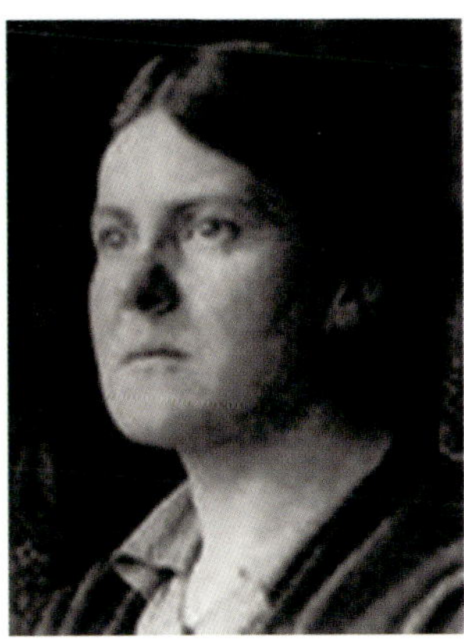

Gwen Raverat (née Gwendolen Mary Darwin) was born in Cambridge, where she lived for most of her life. At the age of nine, she began drawing lessons with Mary Greene, a Parisian-educated painter based in Cambridge. She enrolled at the Slade School of Fine Art in 1908. Even during her time in London, she retained strong links with Cambridge and was a member of the 'neo-pagan' group at the University, which included students such as Rupert Brooke and Virginia Woolf. She later continued her association with these students through the Bloomsbury Group.

Raverat played a fundamental role in modernising the technique of wood engraving in Britain. She was a founding member of the SWE. Between the Society's establishment in 1920, up until 1940, Raverat exhibited 122 engravings. She ceased to produce wood engravings after suffering a stroke in 1951. Raverat was especially interested in children's fiction and most of her book illustrations were produced from the 1930s. Her childhood home is now situated within Darwin College, University of Cambridge (named after her grandfather, the naturalist Charles Darwin).

Rachel Reckitt (1908 -1995)

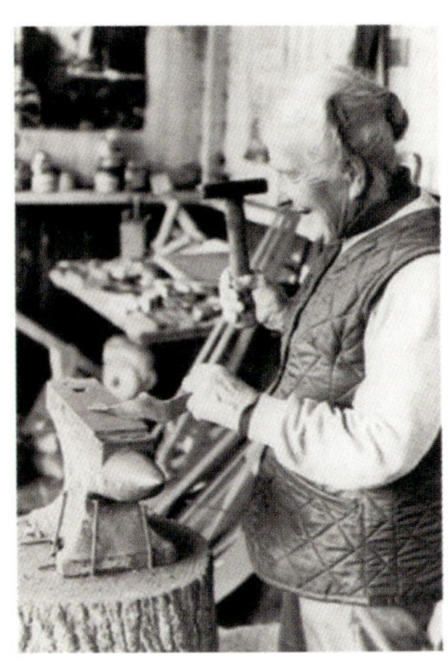

Rachel Reckitt worked in two and three dimensions in mild steel, wood, stone, paint and wood engraving.

Born in St Albans, Hertfordshire, she studied at the Grosvenor School of Modern Art in late 1930s under Iain Macnab, and between 1970-5 at the Roadwater Smithy, Somerset, with Harry and Jim Horrobin. She lived and worked in west Somerset at Rodhuish, Minehead. She carried out commissions for pub signs, wood-engraved book illustrations and sculpture, (including five commissions for Somerset churches). She was an honorary member of the Somerset Guild of Craftsmen and SWE and a member of British Artist Blacksmiths' Association. She exhibited at Wertheim Gallery and LG, had solo exhibitions at Duncan Campbell Contemporary Art and Bridgwater Arts Centre and a retrospective in 2001 at Somerset County Museums, accompanied by a publication: *Rachel Reckitt: Where everything that meets the eye – a retrospective*, by Hal Bishop.

Frances Richards (1903-1985)

Frances Richards (née Clayton) worked as a pottery designer for Paragon while studying at Burslem School of Art (1919-24), before winning a scholarship to the RCA (1924- 27) where she met Ceri Richards (whom she married in 1929).

Greatly influenced by Italian Renaissance painters, she specialised in tempera and fresco painting in her studies, and continued to work in tempera after leaving the college. During the 1930s she produced lithographs, and in 1931 provided twelve drawings for *The Revelation of St. John the Divine*.

In 1945, she held her first solo exhibition at the Redfern Gallery, where she exhibited again in 1949 and 1954. She also took part in shows at Hannover Gallery (1950), the Leicester Galleries (1964 and 1969), the Howard Roberts Gallery, and Holsworthy Gallery (1981).

A respected teacher, Richards held posts at Camberwell School of Art (1928–39) and later Chelsea School of Art (1947-59).

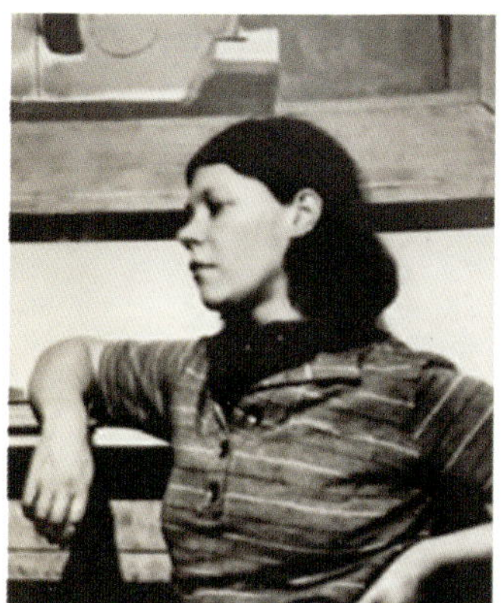

Edith Rimmington (1902-1986)

Edith Rimmington attended the Brighton School of Art (1919-22) where she met fellow artist Leslie Robert Baxter (1893-1986) whom she married in 1926. She joined the British Surrealist Group on relocating to London from Manchester in 1937, and despite being one of its only female members, became a key figure in the movement – showing works at the Surrealist Objects exhibition at the London Gallery (1937) and the International Surrealist Exhibition at the Galerie Maeght in Paris (1947). Much of her work from this time is recognisable for its focus on strange figures and dreams, such as *The Oneiroscopist* (1947).

When the British Surrealist Group disbanded in 1947, Rimmington moved increasingly away from painting to explore Surrealist ideas through automatic poetry and experimental photography.

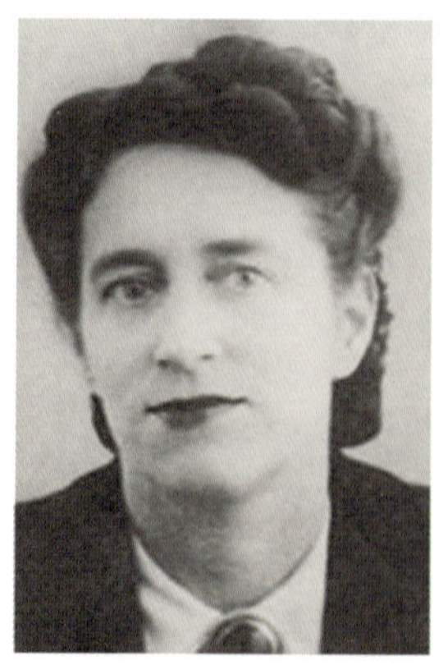

Paule Vézelay (1892-1984)

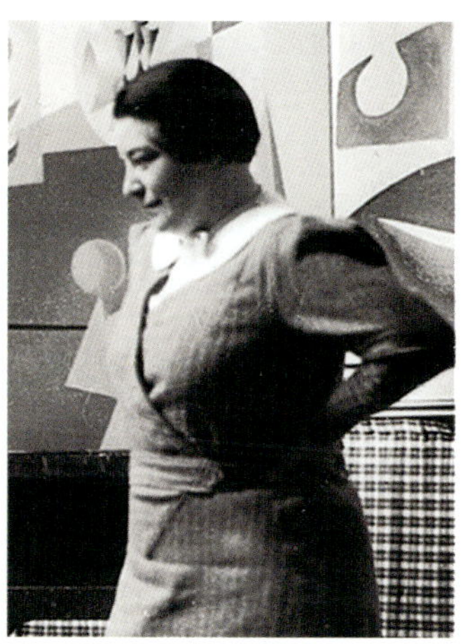

Paule Vézelay (née Marjorie Watson-Williams) studied at Bristol School of Art, London School of Art and Chelsea Polytechnic. She first exhibited in London in 1921 and joined the LG the next year. In 1926, she moved to Paris and adopted the name Paule Vézelay, which – despite the moniker's distinctly French nature – she claimed was "for purely aesthetic reasons".

Closely associated with André Masson (1896-1987) (with whom she lived for four years), Jean Arp (1886-1966) and Sophie Taeuber-Arp (1889-1943) during this period, by the early 1930s Vézelay's work had become increasingly abstract and she joined Abstraction-Création in 1934. One of only a few British members, she was committed to international, non- representational art.

She returned to London at the outbreak of WWII and experimented with new artistic forms, including reliefs, painting and textiles, some of which were shown at the Grosvenor Gallery in 1968. A retrospective exhibition of her work was held at the Tate Gallery in 1983.

Marion Wallace-Dunlop (1864 -1942)

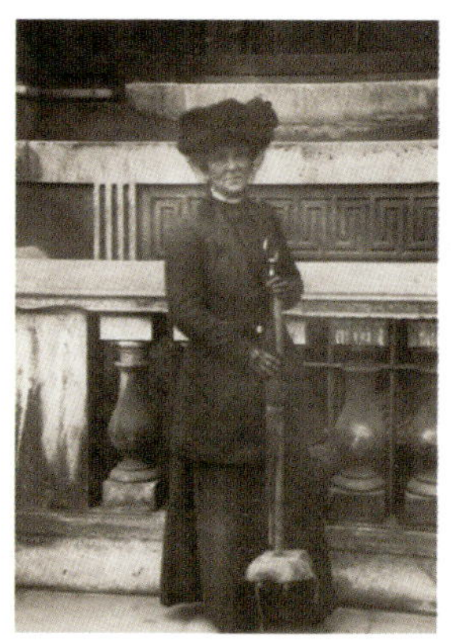

Marion Wallace-Dunlop was a portrait painter, figurative artist, illustrator and ardent feminist. While studying at the Slade School of Fine Art, recognition of her talent resulted in the commissioning, in 1899, of two illustrated books: *Fairies, Elves and Flower Babies* and *The Magic Fruit Garden*. She exhibited with the Paris Salon, the RA (1903, 1905, 1906) and the RGI (1903).

Fiercely devoted to the fight for women's rights, she dedicated much of her career, and life, to the suffrage movement. After joining the Women's Social and Political Union in 1908 she was soon arrested for 'obstruction', and was the first suffragette to go on hunger strike while imprisoned in 1909. She also directed the creation of banners, tapestries and prints to call for women's right to vote, particularly for the 'Women's Coronation Procession' in 1911.

List of Illustrations

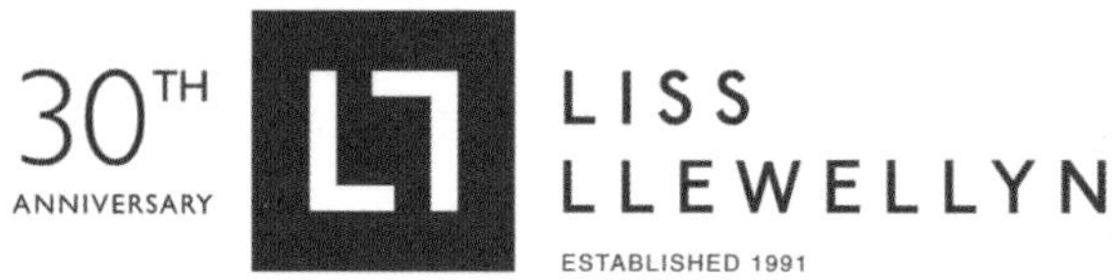

LISS LLEWELLYN

30TH ANNIVERSARY

ESTABLISHED 1991

Founded in 1991 by Paul Liss and Sacha Llewellyn, LISS LLEWELLYN are exhibition organisers, publishers and Fine Art dealers specialising in the unsung heroines and heroes of British art from 1880 to 1980. During the last thirty years LISS LLEWELLYN have worked in association with museums and cultural institutions in the United Kingdom and abroad to develop a series of in-depth exhibitions to encourage the reappraisal of some of the lesser-known figures of twentieth century British art.

EXHIBITIONS

LISS LLEWELLYN exhibitions have been staged at Sir John Soane's Museum (London) / Pallant House Gallery (Chichester) / Cecil Higgins Gallery (Bedford) / Harris Museum (Preston) / Alfred East Gallery (Kettering) / Young Gallery (Salisbury) / Royal Albert Memorial Museum (Exeter) / Royal Museum and Art Gallery (Canterbury) / Fry Art Gallery (Saffron Walden) / Beecroft Art Gallery (Southend) / The Church of England / The British School at Rome.

PUBLICATIONS

LISS LLEWELLYN have published over twenty books on British Art and Artists. Our last four publications have all been longlisted for the Berger Art History Prize. *Alan Sorrell – The Life & Works of an English Neo-Romantic Artist* was chosen as one of the best art books of 2013 by Brian Sewell. *Evelyn Dunbar – The Lost Works* was chosen as one of the best books of 2015 by *The Guardian*.

MUSEUMS

LISS LLEWELLYN sells to museums throughout the UK, in Europe, America, Canada, Australia, and New Zealand. Our clients include:

Tate / The Victoria & Albert Museum / The permanent collection of the House of Commons / The Imperial War Museum / The Science Museum / The British Museum / The National Portrait Gallery / The Fitzwilliam / The Ashmolean / Leeds City Art Gallery / Jerwood Gallery / Southampton Art Gallery / Wolverhampton Art Gallery / Cheltenham Art Gallery / The Ferens City Art Gallery / Scottish National Gallery of Modern Art / Garden Museum (London) / The Hull University Art Collection (Hull) / Williamson Art Gallery and Museum (Birkenhead) / The Bowes Museum (Co. Durham) / Central St Martins Museum and Study Collection / Geffrye Museum (London) / The Whitworth Art Gallery (Manchester) / Metropolitan Museum of New York / Yale Center for British Art / National Gallery of Canada / Le Musée National du Moyen Âge (Paris) / Palazzo Strozzi (Florence) / Art Institute (Chicago) / Wolfsonian Museum (Miami Beach, Florida) / Musée Cluny (Paris) / The Frick Library (New York) / The Museum für Kunst und Gewerbe (Hambourg) / The Gates Foundation

We have gifted work to the following museums:

V&A, British Museum, UCL Art Museum, National Maritime Museum, Ben Uri, Tate Archive, Imperial War Museum, The Garden Museum and The Wolfsonian, Miami. The collection that we created for Laporte in 2000 was the winner of the Corporate Collection of The Year Award.

LISS LLEWELLYN

Adam House, 7-10 Adam Street, London WC2N 6AA

T: (+44) 7973613374   PAUL@LISSLLEWELLYN.COM   SACHA@LISSLLEWELLYN.COM

www.LISSLLEWELLYN.COM